WOMEN OF FAITH™
STUDY GUIDE SERIES

CULTIVATING
CONTENTMENT

FOREWORD BY

LUCI
SWINDOLL

THOMAS NELSON PUBLISHERS
Nashville

Published by Thomas Nelson, Inc., P.O. Box 141000, Nashville, Tennessee, 37214.

Library of Congress Cataloging–in–Publication data is available.

ISBN: 0–7852–51529

Printed in Canada.

04 05 06 07 08–6 5 4

✦ CONTENTS ✦

✦ FOREWORD ✦

If contentment could be weighed, I'd say it's about 90 pounds. That's what Edna weighed soaking wet, and she was a bundle of contentment. Eighty years old, full of spunk, living alone and sharp as a tack, indomitable little Edna ruled the roost in her neighborhood. I was an impressionable young college student when I first met her but in all the years since, I've never met a happier person.

I've thought about Edna a million times. Every time our paths crossed she told me about something that gave her joy. Her latest batch of gorgeous flowers or the stray cat that showed up at her door. Chapters in the Bible she was memorizing. New curtains she bought when she'd saved enough money. I loved this woman! I can't tell you how she lifted my spirits. Edna had kind of a secret formula that I finally figured out—don't compete, don't complain, don't compare. I don't know what age she was when she learned this but by eighty she had it down pat.

Edna's daughter, Marian, and I sang together in the church choir and often she took me with her on Sundays to visit her mom. As we'd walk across the yard, classical music could be heard mixed with the sound of Edna's humming. She had a large library and had read every book in it...some, twice. She could quote Scripture and poetry and whole essays. One time she had me check out her rendition of the Gettysburg Address. She didn't miss a word.

While cultivating her flowerbed, she was also planting seeds of tranquility, peace, and acceptance in her heart. She knew the Savior who had become her friend. She took Him at His word, believing He would be everything she needed. She didn't envy those around her for what they had. When a prosperous developer offered her a huge amount of money for her land, promising a brand new house in a better neighborhood she said, "What do I want with a new house? My neighbors have new houses and they're not happy."

Edna's heart had found contentment because of what she had inside of her. She lived in a little clapboard house in a small town, never traveled more than 500 miles from home, had no car, and little money. But everything she had, I wanted.

This sweet, little woman was the epitome of the Biblical view of contentment. She got excited over simple things. She enjoyed her surroundings and made them beautiful. Her heart wasn't restless. She knew the difference between a mere inconvenience and a major catastrophe and she lived every day like it was her last. She trusted God that life could be enjoyed through a dimension beyond what she could see or feel. She was grateful, playful, truthful, and watchful. Every now and then, I have this feeling I can see her sitting up there in heaven on a star. I just look up and say "Hi, Edna. Thank you."

—Luci Swindoll

✦ INTRODUCTION ✦

How in the world can I be content in all circumstances?
I really don't believe I can, but I'll try. I'll throw my heart
into it and ask the LORD for his help. Hardships, losses,
inconveniences, interruptions, relinquishments—I could
name twenty things I have to work at to find contentment.
Maybe it won't happen in some areas. I don't know.
I do know one thing: If I don't want it, it will never come.

—Luci Swindoll

Far too often, life falls short of perfection and happiness flits just out of reach. A nagging sense of dissatisfaction works its way into our hearts. *This is not what I wanted out of life.* It takes root and grows. *It just isn't fair!* People disappoint us. Our looks disappoint us. Our decisions disappoint us. Our possessions disappoint us. Our expectations disappoint us. Customer service disappoints us. Even the weather disappoints us! Finally, we cannot contain ourselves. We simply have to let others know what we think—just how bad things are. So what do we do? We tell anyone who will listen. We blurt out life's shortfalls, bemoan life's disappointments, and vent our disgruntled feelings over life's unfairness. In short, we complain.

Life *can* be so hard. Life can be so frustrating. Life can be so…so…daily! Women everywhere face disappointments, disarray, downfalls, delays, drawbacks, and doldrums. It's unavoidable. That's life! The trick is to face life's twists and turns with grace. We yearn to be the kind of women who exude contentment—that quality of serene calmness, unflappable cheerfulness, and peaceful acceptance. We want to be content. But that's so *hard* to do!

Contentment doesn't come naturally, and isn't always learned quickly. But it *can* be learned. You can, like Paul, say, "I have learned in whatever state I am, to be content" (Phil. 4:11). There are pitfalls along the way, bad habits have been formed, thoughtless attitudes have taken hold. Would you like to be able to find satisfaction in daily living that cannot be ruffled by circumstances? Would you like to break old habits and learn a new way of looking around you? Come, and allow God to cultivate a heart of contentment in you.

"I've kept my feet on the ground,
I've cultivated a quiet heart.
Like a baby content in its mother's arms,
my soul is a baby content."

Psalms 131:2 MSG

CHAPTER 1

DISCONTENT

"I AM DISGUSTED WITH MY LIFE. LET ME COMPLAIN FREELY.
I WILL SPEAK IN THE BITTERNESS OF MY SOUL."

Job 10:1 NLT

♡

Remember Goldilocks, of the Three Bears fame? It's a little hard to relate to Goldilocks. Sure, she did a little shopping around, a little trial and error, and a little exploration of her options—but in the end, she always hit upon something that was "just right." And by the third try, too! Just right. Have you found that state of complete contentment yet? Or like the rest of us, are you still complaining that what you have is "too hot" or "too cold" or "too soft" or "too hard?"

It's not difficult to spot discontentment in our lives. We are weary of the sameness of things. We like a fresh look. Even something that was "just right" a couple of months ago might need some major renovation when the urge to change hits. Now it's time to 'fess up. Aren't you a frequent

CLEARING
✦ THE ✦
COBWEBS

What kinds of things do you dread shopping for, because it is so hard to find just the right size, color, or fit?

> *Longings. Coming face to face with the fact that there are empty places in our lives that haven't been filled. Yearnings. Wanting more than we have: more love, more enjoyment, more passion, more hope, more rest. Cravings. The hope of finding something that will satisfy the rumbling we feel in the stomach of our soul.*
>
> Nicole Johnson

furniture mover? Don't you often reorganize your pantry or your desk? How many old purses are stuffed onto the back shelf of your closet? Wouldn't you love to trade in your car? Your sofa? Your bedroom curtains?

Where else does this urge to find that "just right" thing crop up? Do you change your mind annually about the wallpaper in your kitchen? Do you change your hair color? How many different colors of paint have been on your bathroom walls? Do you still like the clothes you bought two seasons ago? How many times have you rearranged your office? How long is your to–do list, your shopping list, or your wish list?

We're always looking for ways to eliminate feelings of discontentment gnawing away at our sense of satisfaction. What will you try next? If you try a new schedule, new style, new size, new scenery, new shoes, new scents, or negotiate a new salary, will it do any good?

1. What kinds of things do we look for to satisfy the restlessness in our hearts?

2. The Proverbs are filled with common sense and uncommon wisdom. Even fabulously wealthy King Solomon understood the insatiable nature of people. He said Greed has twin daughters, and their names are "Gimme" and "Gimme more" (30:15 MSG). Consider the lesson recorded in Proverbs 30:15, 16. What four things does Solomon say are never satisfied?

3. There is so much in this world that simply cannot satisfy. Discontent is not a product of modern, commercialized society either. Take a look at what Solomon had to say about people in Ecclesiastes 6:6.

4. This world is tainted by sin, and cannot possibly fulfill the expectations we hold onto. How does Paul describe the state of the world in Romans 8:19–21?

Because we live in a fallen world, we will experience negatives in our lives. Heartache and disappointment will come our way. We experience "stuff" we don't deserve, don't want, and can't send back. It's ours. But thanks be to God, nothing happens in this world that He doesn't know about and that He can't handle.

Thelma Wells

So what recourse do we have? Do we spend our days like Oscar the Grouch, a disgruntled pessimist, trying to throw a wet blanket on everyone who passes? Are we left to stew in our feelings of dissatisfaction, unhappiness, restlessness, and displeasure? Do we succumb to our grumpy tendencies? Do we sigh over sin's hold on a fallen world, helpless to overcome our complaining habits? I don't think so!

5. Are we left desolate—doomed to a life of discontentment? No, we're not. There is more to life than this physical world. Where can we find richness and satisfaction according to Isaiah 55:2?

When we look at the desires of our hearts in light of reality, we know none of them is achievable all the time. They're changeable, like the weather. Some days we're content; others we're not.

Luci Swindoll

6. David agreed God was better than anything in the world. How did he put that thought into words in Psalm 63:5? How did he respond to God's generosity?

7. Food, fun, collections, and connections come and go. What God offers our hearts is unfailing, unfading, and eternal. What does the psalmist ask for in Psalm 90:14?

8. What kind of love does God offer to those who belong to him? Jeremiah 31:3 says it beautifully.

> *You were made for more than this world has to offer you. Our yearnings, longings, cravings, and hopes are telling us something: there isn't enough love, peace, hope, friendship, and intimacy on this earth to completely satisfy us. We will always want more.*
>
> Nicole Johnson

9. In spite of this sinful world, in spite of our nagging discontentment, why do we hang on to our belief in the "fairy tale ending"? Don't we all expect things to work out happily ever after somehow? What does Romans 5:5 say about the hope to which we cling?

✦ DIGGING DEEPER ✦

We have a natural tendency to pursue happiness. We long for contentment, and are willing to explore every avenue available in order to achieve it. Without even realizing it, we sometimes try to fill an emptiness in our lives that only God can satisfy. We cannot satisfy our discontentment by accumulating the things this world has to offer. Here are a few more Scriptures that support this truth.

- Psalm 145:16
- Proverbs 30:8
- Proverbs 23:4
- Ecclesiastes 5:10

✦ PONDER & PRAY ✦

As you face the week ahead, take time to search your heart for signs of discontentment. Ask the Spirit to bring to light the kinds of disappointment that allow bitterness and anger to take root. To what have you been turning in order to satisfy the restlessness in your heart? Pray that you, like David, can discover how God's love can satisfy your heart.

✦ TRINKETS TO TREASURE ✦

At the close of every Women of Faith conference, women are asked to play a little game of pretend. Each conference guest is asked to imagine a gift has been placed in her hands—one from each of the speakers—to serve as reminders of the different lessons shared. This study guide will carry on this tradition! At the close of each lesson, you will be presented with a small gift. Though imaginary, it will serve to remind you of the things you have learned. Think of it as a souvenir. Souvenirs are little trinkets we pick up on our journeys to remind us of where we have been. They keep us from forgetting the path we have traveled. Hide these little treasures in your heart, for as you ponder on them, they will draw you closer to God.

✦ TRINKETS TO TREASURE ✦

Remember Goldilocks? This week's trinket will help remind you of her search for something that was "just right." A teddy bear, in token of the three bears. Life may be too hot, too cold, or too hard at times, but your searching can end today. God can satisfy the longing in your heart, and you can hang on to your hope for a happy ending.

✦ Notes & Prayer Requests ✦

CHAPTER 2

♡

RESTLESS SOULS

"THE SPIRIT OF GOD WHETS OUR APPETITE
BY GIVING US A TASTE OF WHAT'S AHEAD.
HE PUTS A LITTLE OF HEAVEN IN OUR HEARTS
SO THAT WE'LL NEVER SETTLE FOR LESS."

2 Corinthians 5:3–5 MSG

♡

Homesickness. It's the longing for something precious and familiar. It's the sadness that overwhelms us when we are lost and alone. It is a wave of nostalgia, a bittersweet ache, a flood of memories that overtakes us suddenly.

Have you ever been in the middle of something, just puttering around, when suddenly you are transported to a time or place long ago? It doesn't take much. Sometimes it's a sound—the slap of a screen door, the tune an ice cream truck plays, the opening chords of a favorite hymn. Sometimes it's a smell—sawdust, baking bread, or school paste. Sometimes it's a forgotten but familiar

CLEARING
✦ THE ✦
COBWEBS

What smell, sight, or sound brings back pleasant memories of childhood for you?

> *So what is the soul? It is the deepest aspect of ourselves, the spiritual part that cries out for heaven, that is made to be a dwelling place for God. Nothing and no one else can answer that thirst. It is the size of eternity.*
>
> Sheila Walsh

sight—the bedroom you slept in as a child, the album filled with fading snapshots, the campus where you first experienced independence.

But have you ever experienced that homesick feeling for a place you haven't been, or a face you've yet to see? It happens when we are in the middle of something else, and suddenly we are transported. It's the sight of something so beautiful, that it makes us cry. It's that moment in the midst of a worship service when we catch a fleeting glimpse of heaven's glory. It's the thrill of understanding when a passage of Scripture shifts into focus for us. It's the sense of wonder that throbs through us when we see the caring of which the community of Christ is capable. At those moments of homesickness, our yearning for heaven is so intense.

1. Our souls are restless with a longing to see God. How does David describe the state of his heart in Psalm 63:1?

2. We long for God, and we have a Spirit–led urge to seek Him out. What else does our inner self long for, according to Psalm 84:2?

3. Is our hope without its basis? No. We have been assured that our longing to see our Savior will be fulfilled. What did Jesus promise in John 14:2, 3?

4. Imagine that! Jesus the carpenter is working on a new home for us. How does Paul describe the attitude of our hearts in Philippians 3:20?

5. The insults and inadequacies of this world will fade in the light of heaven. How does Paul describe the happy ending we are longing for in 1 Corinthians 2:9?

The human heart quests for satisfaction and keeps at it until it finds some kind of peace in God. Until that day, we say, in effect, "It has to be better over there"—and "over there" can be virtually anywhere. And even when we find contentedness in the LORD and know for a fact that He is our constant companion, it's still difficult for the heart to give up the hunt.

Luci Swindoll

*I*s there a reason why it's so hard to be content? Why is it that nothing on this earth brings us complete satisfaction? Perhaps it's a gift from God. Think about it. Would you really want this broken, sinful world to be the fulfillment of your wildest dreams? Aren't you glad to know something far better awaits us?

6. The reality is this earthly life will never completely satisfy. We weren't made to find complete contentment here. How is this state of affairs described in 2 Corinthians 5:4?

> *Augustine said that our hearts are restless until they rest in God, but we try all sorts of things to still that pounding in our heads and the ache in our souls.*
>
> Sheila Walsh

7. Are we alone in our wait? What else is longing for redemption according to Romans 8:22, 23?

8. Heaven will be perfect. We cannot imagine how good it will be, but God has let us know enough details about it so we can look forward with honest eagerness. What are some of the things we know for sure about heaven from Revelation 21:4 and 22:3?

9. Here is a beautiful verse from the Psalms — one which should be committed to memory. Let' s close our lesson with David's words in Psalm 17:15. When does he say he will be fully satisfied?

✦ Digging Deeper ✦

A song of praise and worship being lifted up in churches today declares, "You are the air I breathe. You are my daily bread...And I am desperate for You." David described his longing for God in terms of thirst. As believers, we are to hunger and thirst after righteousness. Let's look at a few more passages that encourage these appetites.

- Psalm 42:2
- Psalm 143:6
- Psalm 107:9
- John 6:35

✦ Ponder & Pray ✦

Have you been trying to settle yourself happily on this earth, and been frustrated when one thing after another delays your efforts? As you consider the different Scripture passages in this week's lesson, pray that the LORD will stir up your longing for heaven and for Him. We weren't meant to get too comfortable here. Don't be dismayed when you see how far life falls short of your ideals. Thank the LORD for the restlessness in your soul. It helps to remind you that this world is not your true home.

✦ Trinkets to Treasure ✦

There are some things in this life which are wonderful, but leave you wanting more. With this distinctive trait in mind, the trinket for you to treasure this week is one potato chip. Crispy, crunchy, lightly salted—the saying goes that you can't eat just one. So when the taste of your single chip leaves you craving more, let it serve as a reminder of your heart's longing for heaven. For until you see your Savior face to face, you'll never be truly satisfied.

✦ Notes & Prayer Requests ✦

CHAPTER 3

THE COMPLAINER IN ALL OF US

"DON'T I HAVE A RIGHT TO COMPLAIN? WILD DONKEYS BRAY WHEN THEY FIND NO GREEN GRASS, AND OXEN LOW WHEN THEY HAVE NO FOOD."

Job 6:5 NLT

♡

One of the most visible results of a discontented heart comes right out of our mouths. Complaining is a habit we all seem to learn. We start young, and we learn it very well. Nobody needs to teach us how to complain. It comes quite naturally. And nowhere is this gift for gripe more apparent than in children. A child can complain before they even learn how to speak—it's all in their facial expressions. Can't you just see their sweet faces, contorted by narrowed eyes, a furrowed brow, and a protruding lower lip? As children grow, they refine their pouting technique, adding the stamped foot, huffy sigh, the eye roll, and the ever ready wail

CLEARING ✦ THE ✦ COBWEBS

We call our favorite gripes our "pet peeves." What is your pet peeve?

of protest. "Her piece is bigger than mine!" "He took the one I was going to take!" "She always gets to go first!"

As we grow into adulthood, most of us drop our bouts of sulking and we don't stick out our lower lip anymore. But this isn't really a sign that the complaining has ended. We have just refined our style.

1. What kind of complaints do you most often hear?

> *What I'd really like to do when the plane is late or the luggage is lost is get upset—start whining and moaning. Or I want to be mad—raise my voice, harden my heart, tighten up my face, and unload a sharp tongue—lashing to any unfortunate soul who happens to cross my path. But frankly, I've tried those choices, and neither one is satisfying. As quickly as I vent my frustration I regret my thoughtless words and harsh remarks.*
>
> Barbara Johnson

2. Why do people complain about such things? Does it serve any purpose? Does it do any good?

3. Proverbs sheds some light on complaining. To what is a complainer compared in Proverbs 27:3?

4. Job was an amazing complainer. He's really quite famous for his sometimes–whiney monologues. Much of the Book of Job records the outpouring of his heart in the face of personal tragedy. What does he say in Job 10:1? Have you ever felt this way?

5. Have you ever caught yourself complaining over something truly petty, and wondered why in the world it even matters? In times like that, we are complaining more because it feels better to be venomous than to have an actual grievance to air. Job makes a trifling complaint in Job 6:6. What is his problem in that verse?

> *My most painful experiences have given me my greatest strength and fiber—what I most needed to mature. Through them I was forced to rely on the LORD, deal with reality for what it was, defer reward—in short, quit griping and grow up! The very things I hated have been the making of me.*
>
> Luci Swindoll

There are lots of ways to describe us when discontentment boils over: cranks, whiners, grumps, moaners, groaners, gripers, snipers, mopers, sulkers, wasps, and shrews. We get ornery, squirrelly, peevish, owlish, snappish, crabby, and edgy.

You know the type—sort of like Eeyore, the gloomy donkey of Winnie the Pooh® fame. No matter what cheerful circumstance he and his friends are in, Eeyore's melancholy mindset makes his ears and tail droop ever lower. A complaining woman can always find something to gripe about. Point out the sun in the sky, and they complain about sunburn, the lack of rain, and the ozone. Take them out for coffee, and they complain about the overabundance of choices on the menu, the exorbitant costs, the inattentiveness of the waitress. Bring them a bouquet of flowers, and they complain about pollen allergies, the fleeting nature of cut flowers, and the fact that they don't receive flowers often enough.

6. Are there different kinds of complaining? Is some complaining socially acceptable—like a form of small talk? Does acceptability make it okay?

People may not be aware of all my internal struggles, because I've learned, through much practice, to resist dumping the whole truck on some unsuspecting victim.

Luci Swindoll

7. "If you don't have anything nice to say, don't say anything at all!" That was one of my Dad's pet phrases. It was his way of trying to get my sister and me to curb our tongues. But are there times when our complaints can be heard without condemnation?

Let's compare a couple of complaints. First, consider the parable of Jesus in Matthew 20: 1–16. What was the response of the workers to the owner of the field in Matthew 20:11?

When our son, Tim, was killed by a drunk driver...I needed to grieve. I would drive alone at night to a dump a few miles away. There I would sob, and sometimes even scream. This was my way of venting emotions that had to be released.

Barbara Johnson

8. All right. Now take a look at a complainer in 1 Samuel 1:12–17. Why is this woman upset?

9. What is the difference between complaining about your troubles to God and complaining about those same things to the people around you?

✦ Digging Deeper ✦

Consider this verse, as it is translated in *The Message*:

As long as you grab for what makes you feel good or makes you look important, are you really much different than a babe at the breast, content only when everything's going your way? — 1 Corinthians 3:3

What kind of contentment does this verse talk about? Is this the kind of contentment you wish to cultivate?

How is this verse in contrast to the Theme Verse at the opening of this book — Psalm 131:2?

✦ PONDER & PRAY ✦

This week, pray that the Spirit will help you to put a watch on your tongue. Ask God to help you see His perspective on the comments that come out of your mouth. Have you been thoughtlessly complaining? Redirect your disappointments and grievances to the LORD this week, and see if He doesn't listen and act on your behalf.

✦ TRINKETS TO TREASURE ✦

Do you like a combination of sweet and sour? The two tastes compliment each other so well — the tartness of the sour taking an edge off the cloying sweetness, the sweetness taking the pucker out of the sour. This week's trinket will serve to remind us that we must seek balance in our lives, and above all, avoid becoming sour in our spirits. Take a handful of Sweet Tarts this week, and remember — though we can't always be sweet, we can sweeten our sourest thoughts with the LORD's help.

✦ Notes & Prayer Requests ✦

✦ NOTES & PRAYER REQUESTS ✦

CHAPTER 4

CONSTANT DRIP

"A NAGGING WIFE ANNOYS LIKE A CONSTANT DRIPPING."

Proverbs 19:13 NLT

♡

id you want to be an artist when you grew up? I know I did. Well, my mother is an artist—for real. She's a watercolorist, and has opened a gallery in the little Scandinavian town where I grew up—it's called Countryside Arts. Whenever I go home to visit, Mom shows me all her newest pieces, and I ooh and aah over them. Inevitably, there will be one painting that will leap off the walls. I'll put dibbs on it, and drag out my checkbook. So far, I have five of my Mom's paintings on my walls at home. But my favorite has to be my most recent purchase. It's called "Constant Drip."

It's a painting of the faucet over the bathtub in the old farmhouse where I spent my childhood. It shows the old–fashioned knobs and a slightly cockeyed spout

CLEARING
✦ THE ✦
COBWEBS

What kinds of things leak? List all the things that come to mind!

> *Some people spread joy wherever they go—whether or not they mean to! And some of us have to put forth a little effort to keep a smile in our hearts. Others are never happy unless they're complaining about something.*
>
> Barbara Johnson

against white tile. The morning sun catches the glass bottles of bubble bath, the ring on the white rubber stopper for the drain, and on the single drop of water that glistens on the verge of release. "Constant Drip" is the perfect title, because over the years, that tub has known the infrequent plinking of water.

Now it hangs over my bathtub, and serves as a dual reminder for me. It reminds me of my childhood home, capturing something both mundane and precious to me. But the painting's second purpose is to serve as a reminder to my heart of that verse in Proverbs: "A continual dripping on a very rainy day and a contentious woman are alike" (Prov. 27:15). As the woman of the house, how am I conducting myself? Am I making our house a place of welcome and peace, or am I a source of frustration and annoyance for those closest to me?

1. Complainers really can be tiresome people! Are you making yourself as tiresome as the woman found in Proverbs 19:13 and 27:15? Look up those verses in as many translations as possible to get the fullest picture of her personality. What words are used to describe her?

2. How does a woman set the temperature in her home? How can she affect the moods of those around her?

3. Let's take a look at another Proverb about cranky women. Turn to Proverbs 21:19. What does Solomon pass along as wise advice for his son?

4. Would you say Proverb 21:19 might occasionally apply to you? Do you want it to?

5. I have known women whose steady whining made them unwelcome companions. An hour in their presence was so draining, I'd feel exhausted by the time we parted ways. Do you enjoy the company of a complainer? Why not?

> *Whiners neither enjoy nor give joy. But grace–filled people are reputable, sought after, and deeply loved.*
>
> Patsy Clairmont

6. Women who choose their friends unwisely can find themselves feeding off each other's urge to complain. In Proverbs 13:20, what does Solomon say about the care needed in choosing your companions?

*I*t only takes a slow, steady dripping to make a woman disagreeable company. The remarks may be small, but they come constantly. Their repetitious patter is distracting, invasive, and maddening. We can become a kind of byword—a party pooper, a wet blanket, a sour note, a sad sack, a dash of cold water, a bitter pill, a gloomy gus, a leaky faucet. Those close to us find themselves longing for escape. Are people looking for reasons to avoid you—to get away from you? Or are you pleasant company, rain or shine?

7. Why does James say we should avoid complaining about one another? It's in James 5:9.

A calmer faith—that's the quiet place within us where we don't get whiplash every time life tosses us a curve. When we don't revolt when His plan and ours conflict. Where we relax (verses stew, sweat, and swear) in the midst of an answerless season. Where we accept (and expect) deserts in our spiritual journey as surely as we do joy.

Patsy Clairmont

8. A woman holds within her the God–given ability to influence the people around her. She has the ability to smooth things over and the ability to stir things up. In Timothy 1:5, how did two women in the New Testament use their feminine abilities in their home?

9. God has given all believers spiritual gifts. But why did our Heavenly Father give women such a strong influence within our own circles? What has God asked us to do with these gifts, according to 1 Peter 4:10?

✦ DIGGING DEEPER ✦

Nagging, complaining, and other signs of a lack of contentment can wear a person down. Let's take a look at the flip side now. What does the Bible have to say about taking a cheerful approach to life?

- Proverbs 12:25
- Proverbs 15:13, 15
- Proverbs 15:30
- 1 Thessalonians 5:16

✦ PONDER & PRAY ✦

As you consider how this week's lesson applies to you, ask yourself a question: What kind of effect are you having on your family, your co-workers, your friends, and even strangers? Pray that God will open your eyes to the subtle damage your tongue can do. Ask God to help you use your influence to create an atmosphere around you that would please Him.

✦ Trinkets to Treasure ✦

Your trinket this week will serve as a reminder that you don't want to become a drip—a medicine dropper! Even in the smallest of doses, nagging and complaining make people want to turn heels and run. None of us wants to make a nuisance of ourselves. Let your dropper remind you to take care with your words. Measure them with love, peace, and encouragement instead.

✦ Notes & Prayer Requests ✦

CHAPTER 5

THE VERDICT

"HOW LONG SHALL I BEAR WITH THIS EVIL
CONGREGATION WHO COMPLAIN AGAINST ME?"

Numbers 14:27

♡

et's recap here. We are a people with restless souls, unable to find true contentment until we see our Savior face to face. Many of us choose to face these twinges of discontent with an irritability that sharpens our tongues. So we complain. We all agree that complaining doesn't serve any good purpose. When we vent our frustrations to those around us, it sours their attitudes. It breeds the urge to complain in others. It's a thoughtless habit we pass along to our families.

This is all very reasonable—common sense, really. But wait! Stop! Hit the brakes! Hold that thought! We have not yet addressed one vital perspective. Consider for a moment: What does *God* think about our complaining tongues?

CLEARING
✦ THE ✦
COBWEBS

If your food fell from heaven like manna, and you could gather up as much as you wanted every day, what kind of food would you want?

> *What Christ cares about is our hearts, our complete love and devotion. And He will create crisis in our lives to show us what holds us.*
>
> Sheila Walsh

1. The best place to start for this consideration is in the desert. When Moses led the Israelites out of Egypt, he had no idea what a long and bumpy ride was ahead of him. Even with miraculous intervention, the people found reasons to murmur. What kinds of things did they complain about in Numbers 21:5?

2. Moses got the brunt of all the peoples' complaints, but who were the Israelites really complaining about? Read Exodus 16:7 to find out.

3. Even Job admitted to his listeners, "It's not you I'm complaining to — it's God" (Job 21:4 MSG). How does the Bible describe these heaven-bound complaints? Both Exodus 17:2 and Deuteronomy 6:16 give us God's perspective of them.

4. God is patient. God is longsuffering. God is merciful. But the children of Israel's unbelievable ingratitude finally brings on some consequences. What happens in Numbers 11:1?

5. Even after some serious chastisement, the Israelites continue to whine and complain. This time, God teaches them a lesson by giving them exactly what they ask for. What does the LORD say in Numbers 11:20?

6. Those who continue to flaunt their disobedience in the face of God will suffer the consequences. What is the final verdict over the murmuring masses in Numbers 14:29?

If my mind becomes cluttered by the day's annoyances, it's a given that sooner or later I'm going to lose my self–control. If I lose my self–control, for sure I'm going to lose my joy. I hate losing my joy. Fortunately, I have a choice how I react.

Marilyn Meberg

Every parent or nursery worker has faced the struggle of trying to calm a cranky child. There are those children who are simply looking for comfort. They will clutch a teddy bear, take a pacifier, melt into a warm hug, and consent to be rocked to sleep. But little can be done for the child who does not wish to be comforted. Some are screamers, shrilly announcing their displeasure to the world. Some are soft weepers, with down–turned mouths and steady streams of tears coursing from their wide, sad eyes. Some are kickers, twisting and lashing out at anyone who tries to comfort them. Some are sulkers, and they withdraw themselves to a corner or under a table to wait out their ordeal.

When your Heavenly Father finds you in a cranky mood, are you ready for His comforting embrace? Do you allow His love to melt away the tension, the disappointments, and the anger? Or are you like the strong–willed child, lashing out against His gentle touch or withdrawing for a long, lonely sulk?

7. How would you describe the attitude of the children of Israel in the desert?

8. Did the Israelites have any basis for their grievances? Much later, Isaiah challenges the complaints of God's people. What does he say in Isaiah 40:27?

9. Are we in the same boat? How often do we complain, revealing a forgetful, childish, selfish heart? Take a few moments and list some of the things God has done in your life, leaving you with nothing to complain about.

✦ DIGGING DEEPER ✦

We have considered the complaints of Job, and followed the murmurings of the children of Israel. Now take a little time to look at another petulant prophet — Jonah. Read Jonah 4:1–4 and consider the following questions. Why is Jonah upset with God? What would Jonah have rather seen done? Does Jonah have any right to try and thwart God's plans? Does Jonah have any right to be angry? Is Jonah's sulking doing any good, or is he just setting himself up as a stubborn and ridiculous figure? Do you ever have Jonah days?

✦ PONDER & PRAY ✦

Have you ever considered that complaining springs from an ungrateful heart? When you gripe about petty things, did you know you are complaining against God Himself? Confess to the LORD your shortcomings in this area of your life. This week, as you pray, ask the Spirit to open your eyes to all of God's blessings in your life. Ask Him for a changed perspective so you can see the good in whatever situation you encounter.

✦ TRINKETS TO TREASURE ✦

Our complaining mouths only highlight the ungrateful attitudes pervading our hearts. This week's trinket will serve to remind you that childish sulking and selfishness must be set aside. Most of us wouldn't dream of putting a pacifier in our mouth, but your new pacifier will be very useful. When you come down with a plague of selfishness and sulking, pop in your pacifier, and send up a desperate prayer for a change of heart.

✦ NOTES & PRAYER REQUESTS ✦

✦ NOTES & PRAYER REQUESTS ✦

CHAPTER 6

WHAT'S THE ALTERNATIVE?

"IN EVERYTHING YOU DO, STAY AWAY FROM COMPLAINING AND ARGUING."

Philippians 2:14 NLT

♡

In the small, Midwestern town where I grew up, there were a lot of little catch phrases people used. Some make me smile when I think of them, like "you betcha" and "ufda." Others can be mildly frustrating, like "whatever," or "it could be worse." But my favorite old–timer phrase is a real staple—"Can't complain."

What a useful phrase! For instance, how do you respond to the usual "Hi, how are you?" Do you say "good," "fine," "hanging in there," "just great," "couldn't be better," or "swell"? Why not try "can't complain" for a while? That's how it is used in my hometown. It also comes in handy in conversations about the weather.

CLEARING ✦ THE ✦ COBWEBS

What kinds of words or phrases were in vogue when you were in high school or college?

"Been getting enough rain over your way?" "Can't complain." Or how about inquiries about your health? "How's your back holding out these days?" "Can't complain." If you start all your conversations with this little phrase, you'll be reminded to take your own advice, and not complain! It'll give your attitude of gratitude a little nudge in the right direction.

1. Are there times when we should simply curb our tongues? What does Solomon say in Proverbs 29:11?

There is so much in life that is wonderful, and it's not too late to grab hold of it. It's not too late to be kind, it's not too late to be loving, it's not too late to tell the truth, to be honest. It's not too late to pray, it's not too late to tell your children that you love them, it's not too late to tell the LORD that you love Him.

Sheila Walsh

2. Here's another verse on that same theme. What does David urge in Psalm 4:4? For an interesting perspective, compare your own Bible translation with that given by *The Message*.

3. Do you get the impression there's a line being crossed here? When do our frustrated feelings become sin? How does Proverbs 21:23 put this fact into words?

4. James warns us about the trouble our tongues can get us into. What does he say in James 3:2?

5. Does this mean we should pretend to be happy all the time, putting on a false smile no matter what is going on in our hearts?

> *There is no life without pain. No treasure without the hunt...Getting things easily will never make us into the women God is calling us to be.*
>
> Nicole Johnson

o you remember Eddie Haskell? He was one of the neighborhood kids on *Leave It to Beaver*. What a little weasel! We all knew he had a mean streak, but he could turn wide–eyed and innocent whenever the grownups came around. It was infuriating to watch him in action. Keep in mind that contentment is not an Eddie Haskell sham—pasting on a cheerful demeanor, no matter what you may be thinking and feeling underneath.

As with anything in life, contentment requires learning to balance. You can't assume that, because life will never be perfect on earth, you can stomp around telling everybody so. Likewise, you cannot assume that, because life will never be perfect on earth, you can never find contentment.

God promises it is here for us. We just need to find it, and learn to live it.

6. What is the "cure" for the complainer according to Isaiah 29:24?

> *Learning to be content is an educational process, as is all learning. It takes time, and I'm sure over time at least some measure of contentment would come. It would start with the acceptance of present reality and hopefully move toward genuine contentment.*
>
> Luci Swindoll

7. Contentment involves teachability and gratitude! How did Paul "get" contentment, according to Philippians 4:11?

8. How does the Bible rate contentment? Paul gives it high marks in 1 Timothy 6:6.

9. Dissatisfaction and complaining are not unavoidable. There is an alternative—contentment. That Timothy 6:6 passage seems to indicate that it goes hand in hand with godliness—"godliness with contentment." Having both is better than great riches (1 Tim. 6:6 KJV). What is it about contentment that makes godliness better? And why would you want a godly life in which to find contentment?

> *I have learned that to yearn and to learn are quite different. One takes much less effort and a lot less risk than the other.*
>
> Patsy Clairmont

✦ DIGGING DEEPER ✦

Many of us are familiar with Isaiah's cry of dismay, "Woe is me, for I am undone" (Is. 6:5). Let's take a closer look at Isaiah's words as they are translated in *The Message*:

I said, "Doom! It's Doomsday! I'm as good as dead! Every word I've ever spoken is tainted—blasphemous even! And the people I live with talk the same way, using words that corrupt and desecrate. And here I've looked God in the face! The King! God—of—the—Angel—Armies!" —Isaiah 6:5

Why is Isaiah upset? What does he regret? What has made him realize the error of his past ways? Do you think you will be similarly dismayed someday, when faced with a holy God? What does Matthew 12:36 say?

✦ PONDER & PRAY ✦

Pray this week for the Spirit to help you and your tongue stay out of trouble when you get frustrated. Ask for a teachable heart and a grateful outlook, so God can continue to cultivate contentment in your heart.

✦ TRINKETS TO TREASURE ✦

This week's little treasure is small, but will serve as an effective reminder for you. It's a button, and whenever you look at it, remember to "button your lip" when the time is right! If you have trouble, as I sometimes do, in keeping your comments to yourself, you may need more than one! I keep them as magnets on my fridge, glued to tacks for my bulletin board, and in my change purse. Where will you keep your reminders?

✦ NOTES & PRAYER REQUESTS ✦

CHAPTER 7

A WAY OF SEEING

"FINALLY, BRETHREN, WHATEVER THINGS ARE TRUE,
WHATEVER THINGS ARE NOBLE, WHATEVER THINGS ARE
JUST, WHATEVER THINGS ARE PURE, WHATEVER THINGS
ARE LOVELY, WHATEVER THINGS ARE OF GOOD REPORT,
IF THERE IS ANY VIRTUE AND IF THERE IS ANYTHING
PRAISEWORTHY—MEDITATE ON THESE THINGS."

Philippians 4:8

♡

One of the best ways to cultivate contentment in your life is to change the way you look at things. By way of illustration, let me relate a story I'll never forget. A pastor's wife was out calling on a few women in her church. Some of the young, stay–at–home moms in the congregation had expressed interest in having the older, wiser woman meet with them one–on–one. So, the pastor's wife donned a fresh dress, and pearls, and set out. Her first stop found her in front of a tiny two–bedroom home not far from the church building. Balls and tricycles littered

CLEARING
✦ THE ✦
COBWEBS

Is there
something you
collect or love,
and whenever you
go shopping, you notice
it everywhere?

> *Each day the LORD gives us brings with it a reason to rejoice.*
>
> Thelma Wells

the front yard, and the screaming laughter of children could be heard from the open windows of the house. When the door opened after her knock, a sheepish young mother invited her in. The younger woman had completely forgotten about their appointment, and the house was in its customary disarray. Dishes were piled in the sink, the couch cushions were askew, and Cheerios" littered the carpet. Library books were scattered in one corner and building blocks in the other. The blushing homemaker pulled at her stained t–shirt and tried to scrape play dough away from a place at the kitchen table so the pastor's wife would be able to sit. In the midst of all the mess and confusion, the older woman noticed a vase of flowers and exclaimed with genuine pleasure, "Oh my! What a beautiful bouquet of roses! Such lovely blooms! Are they for a special occasion?"

This woman didn't get upset about having her appointment forgotten. She wasn't put off by the mess and noise around her. She surveyed the home, but focused in on the beautiful thing in the middle of the mess. We need to do the same thing—look for the good, right, and lovely things in the midst of chaos.

1. How are you at looking on the bright side, or finding the silver lining?

2. Your way of seeing life hinges on a couple of foundational facts. First of all, do you believe God has a purpose for you? What does Jeremiah 29:11 say?

3. Secondly, your perspective on life is sharpened when you remember that even your trials have a purpose in your spiritual growth. How does Jesus' younger brother describe their usefulness in James 1:2–4?

4. Contentment depends largely on how much you trust God. Seeing life from His perspective helps us to keep our perspective. Do you recall all the disappointments and tragedies that filled the life of Joseph? If anyone could have raised the cry of "unfair!" it was he. But what perspective did he hold on to in Genesis 50:20?

I'm convinced that the whole world is better when we, as individuals, capture and savor each moment as the gift that it is, embrace the challenge or joy of it, and thereby transform it with the magic of creative possibility. Life, for the most part, is what we make it. We have been given a responsibility to live it fully, joyfully, completely, and richly, in whatever span of time God grants us on this earth.

Luci Swindoll

5. Contentment depends on how you approach life, and how you react to what life brings your way. At times, life is good. How does Solomon describe the gift of a good life in Ecclesiastes 5:19, 20?

6. At other times, life is hard. Read Job 2:7–10. What had become of Job's life, and what was he determined to do?

Even when we've landed with our faces in the dust, even when we are caught in a wringer, we can always have hope. And even when hope is lost, it can be regained; we can refocus our perspective.

Barbara Johnson

ave you ever experienced a house fire? We have friends who did. They woke up in the night to the smell of smoke, and hurried to escape through of a bedroom window. Their house burned to the ground and they lost everything—clothing, jewelry, furniture, dishes, collections, family heirlooms, books, artwork, photo albums, financial records, Bibles, toys, souvenirs, trophies, stereo systems, computers, and music. The accumulation of nearly twenty years of married life, with all the paraphernalia that comes with raising a family—all gone in a matter of minutes.

Yet throughout the long ordeal of rebuilding a home, replacing the necessities of life, and making do without the familiar comforts of home, this couple was constant in their thankfulness to God. They were content with what they had because they were grateful for what they had *not* lost—their four children.

7. What is the better thing, according to Proverbs 17:1?

I know I want to be more than I am today. That means I'll have to use my time wisely, invest myself discerningly, and savor the flavor of every delicious moment assigned to me.

Patsy Clairmont

8. Though everything else in life may fail, where is our source of contentment—our source of joy—according to Habakkuk 3:17–19?

9. How can this new way of viewing things be a blessing to those around us? If you look at Romans 12:10–18, you can make a list! How does Paul urge us to reach out to those we see all around us?

✦ DIGGING DEEPER ✦

There is a praise chorus that begins, "Open the eyes of my heart, LORD." When we ask the LORD to give us a new way of seeing things, we are admitting to Him that we have been blind. Often, we are blind to things that have been in front of us all along. We just need fresh eyes to see them. Here are a few more Scripture passages that tell of opened eyes.

- Genesis 21:19
- 2 Kings 6:17
- Numbers 22:31
- Psalm 119:18

✦ PONDER & PRAY ✦

Your prayer this week can echo that of the psalmist, "Open my eyes, that I may see wondrous things from Your law" (Ps. 119:18). Ask God to strengthen your faith as you study His Word. He can give you the tenacity to hold on to hope no matter what circumstances bring. Ask Him to open your eyes to those around you. Your contentment in Christ can be a source of encouragement to others as well.

✦ Trinkets to Treasure ✦

Your trinket to treasure this week is a gift that challenges your way of seeing things—a lemon! To some, a lemon means a poor automobile selection, a sour bite, or a patent pucker. Few people will sit down to peel and enjoy eating a lemon outright. But there are those of us who love lemons, because we know how to deal with them. We can take the lemons of life and make lemonade, lemon bars, and lemon poppy seed cake! Let your friends help you find a new way of loving lemons this week!

✦ Notes & Prayer Requests ✦

✦ NOTES & PRAYER REQUESTS ✦

CHAPTER 8

KEEPING YOUR FOCUS

"GIVE MY SON SOLOMON AN UNCLUTTERED
AND FOCUSED HEART SO THAT HE CAN OBEY
WHAT YOU COMMAND, AND LIVE
BY YOUR DIRECTIONS AND COUNSEL."

1 Chronicles 29:19 MSG

♡

I love pretty things. I love colorful things. But when it comes to pulling on my jeans and putting up my hair every morning, I run into trouble. You see, I lack the feminine gift for fussing. I don't like to fuss over my hair. I rarely paint my nails. I don't wear much jewelry. Unless I'm leaving the house for some reason, I don't even bother with makeup.

I'm not sure where I got left out of the loop in all this stuff. I see other women, and they look so great! They have coordinated outfits, cute shoes, bright lipstick, painted toenails, adorable purses, shining hair, and bold jewelry. Magnificent specimens of femininity, every one of them. But

CLEARING
✦ THE ✦
COBWEBS

What's your favorite accessory?

all of that takes a certain amount of planning and upkeep. Not that I haven't tried. The cupboards in my bathroom are well stocked with baskets of nail polish and lipstick (which I don't use). I have a smattering of hats, purses, scarves, and jewelry (which I also don't use). I even got my ears pierced (at least earrings don't get in my way).

Then, I hit upon the perfect solution for all my accessorizing needs. Sunglasses. I can't go without a pair of sunglasses on a sunny day, so why not coordinate my outfits with different colors of sunglasses! So far, I have pale blue, deep purple, golden brown, and soft pink shades. One day, I found a pale aqua sundress, so I took it over to the sunglasses section and felt positively triumphant when I matched them up with some deep turquoise glasses.

It's easy to be distracted by what other women wear, do, have, and say. We want to fit in so badly. In order to find contentment, we need to find God's niche for us, no matter what everyone else is doing. Then, when we feel God's pleasure in the path we have chosen, it becomes all–important to keep our focus there.

I don't know about you, but I'm susceptible to viewing the lives of others from afar and believing their existence is easier, calmer, and more meaningful than mine— rather paradisiacal. Not all the time, mind you, but I have those moments when I give way to envy because I'm trudging through a dreary season while someone else seems to be skipping down a well–lit path.

Patsy Clairmont

1. Sometimes we are intimidated by those around us. We think one woman has it all together, or some other woman is being used more greatly by God. While others seem to exude grace, poise, wisdom, and contentment, we are struggling to cover the basics. What does the Bible remind us in Job 33:6?

> *Whether you're climbing mountains or think you have a firm grip on everything that's important to you, you would be wise to look to the LORD. Remain humble and aware that your footing could slip at any time. We're on the way to glory land, but we ain't there yet!*
>
> Thelma Wells

2. If we aren't supposed to be distracted by those around us, then where should our focus be? In Philippians 3:8–16, what is Paul focused on?

3. How do we maintain that focus? In 1 Timothy 4:13, what does Paul encourage his son in the faith to concentrate on?

4. To what does Peter compare the Word of God in 2 Peter 1:19?

5. What does David commit himself to do in Psalm 119:112?

6. Solomon urges us on to a similar commitment in Proverbs 4:21. What does he tell us to do with God's Word?

As we meditate on God's Word, we become familiar with God's heart and His ways; as we do so, we will change. The purpose of meditation is not simply to make us feel good in a noisy world; it is not a self–absorbed agenda. Rather, as we shut in our mind with God and reflect on His words, we will know Him and be changed by Him—and that is the purpose of our lives.

Sheila Walsh

There are some things that are really hard to do at the same time as something else. The classic example would be patting your head and rubbing your tummy. Let's see what else fits into that category? Laughing and keeping a straight face. Wearing white and eating spaghetti. Pouting and raising your eyebrows. Eating saltine crackers and whistling. And the ultimate impossible combination—focusing on Jesus and keeping track of everyone else.

7. Unfortunately, focusing on other people is not the only pitfall we can tumble into. Where else do we find our attention drawn according to Philippians 2:3?

8. Keep your eyes on Christ. He's keeping His eyes on you! What does Paul tell us in Ephesians 1:4?

9. Jesus is your example. What does He tell you in John 13:15?

> *When we realize there's no shortcut to having what we want, life gets a bit easier. Not problem free, but definitely easier. We quit thinking that life somehow owes us a living. We work. We pray. We study. We put first things first. We believe God means what He says. Unless we live out these truths, there really is no tomorrow. Everything becomes one endless, tedious, tiresome "today," and there's no growth or change.*
>
> Luci Swindoll

✦ DIGGING DEEPER ✦

Jesus is our pattern—even when it comes to cultivating contentment. That is where our focus should stay when we are shaping our lives. Let's look at a few more New Testament passages that reveal patterns after which we should be modeling our life.

- Philippians 3:17
- 2 Timothy 1:13
- 1 Timothy 1:16
- Titus 2:7

✦ PONDER & PRAY ✦

When we are searching for contentment in our lives, we are easily derailed by our tendency to compare our lives to those around us. To take another step in cultivating the contentment quotient in your heart, pray for the ability to focus your attention on Jesus instead. He is your source of contentment, and He is your pattern for living contentedly. Make an effort to pour over the gospels this week, and commit some of Jesus' teachings to memory.

✦ TRINKETS TO TREASURE ✦

Whenever my mother was marking a pattern, she would pull this wonderful, flat, square piece of blue chalk out of her sewing basket. With this she'd lightly mark the seams. Since our pattern to follow is Jesus, your trinket this week is something for you to use to mark His Word—a blue highlighter. Study His example as you study your Bible, and highlight the portions you want to "keep in the midst of your heart." This will help you keep your focus.

✦ Notes & Prayer Requests ✦

✦ NOTES & PRAYER REQUESTS ✦

CHAPTER 9

THE SOURCE OF CONTENTMENT

"O MY SOUL, YOU HAVE SAID TO THE LORD, 'YOU ARE MY LORD, MY GOODNESS IS NOTHING APART FROM YOU.'"

Psalm 16:2

♡

When I lived up north, I knew where to find what I needed. I knew where the best restaurants were, where to find the best deals on furniture, and where to find cute shoes. I knew where to go when I needed gift–wrap or when I needed fresh flowers. Pumpernickel bagels, pretzels shaped like letters of the alphabet, spices by the ounce, polished rocks, used books, galvanized pails, hat boxes, hothouse poinsettias, and baby ducks. Whether commonplace or obscure, I had my resources.

When I moved south, and found myself plunged into complete darkness. I'd think to myself, "I should really get some of

CLEARING ✦ THE ✦ COBWEBS

Do you have a special shopping spot, where you can get those unique items that aren't available just anywhere?

those cookie cutters shaped like cows and pigs," then realize that I didn't know where to find them here. It'll take me a while to find all those special little shops, now that I live in a new city. After all, to get what you need, you need to know your sources. Without that knowledge, you're sunk!

Do you know your sources, when it comes to spiritual things, like contentment?

1. Contentment, like all the other good gifts showered down on us, come from God. Many Scripture passages acknowledge He is our Source — the Source of what, according to Isaiah 45:24?

I usually don't spend much time thinking about heaven. In fact, when a longing for heaven surfaced, it was a surprise to me. It didn't dawn on me that we hold eternity in our hearts and that would mean we would feel a homesickness in our souls.

Nicole Johnson

2. What is another thing God is the source of, according to David in Psalm 43:4?

3. And according to Psalm 119:114, God's Word is the source of what?

4. Paul also spoke of God as a source for us. What did he say of the Father in 2 Corinthians 1:3?

5. The passage in the previous question declares the Holy Spirit as a source for us. What does He bring into our lives, according to the same verse?

> *When you welcome God's companionship in the darkest hours of your life, when you keep on walking by faith on the darker parts of the path, you are gifted with moments of wonderful elation—as if you are joining with heaven in a celebration that is a tiny shadow of what it will be like when we get home.*
>
> Sheila Walsh

My son has a blankie, and it is a source of great comfort to him. It's a rather posh blankie—a baby gift from an upscale children's store. Even though it is a hand–me–down from an older brother, and has been washed innumerable times, it looks like new. It's not an everyday kind of blankie, though. It's a trippie blankie. In other words, it stays in the van, next to his car seat. Whenever our family gets ready for a trippie (any kind of short–distance car ride), my boy straps himself in, grabs up his precious blankie, and pops his finger in his mouth. When my husband and I crane our necks to make sure every child is safely buckled in, we can't help but smile at this little guy. He's the picture of contentment.

When your journey gets long, do you have a source of comfort?

6. Do we sometimes try to find substitutes for Jesus—other sources of contentment? What do you find yourself leaning on?

Christ offers us daily assistance, divine opportunities, and eternal provision. He also extends to us His Word, which allows us to arch over the world's distorted mindset to receive the pure wisdom that is from above.

Patsy Clairmont

7. How does Ephesians 4:15, 16 describe Jesus in relation to His people?

8. Paul hits this very theme again in Colossians 2:19. How does he describe the activities of Christ in our lives in this passage?

9. Take a look at this verse from Isaiah:

"We're in no hurry, God. We're content to linger in the path sign-posted with your decisions. Who you are and what you've done are all we'll ever want." —Isaiah 26:8 MSG

According to Isaiah, what is our source of contentment, and how do we behave because of that?

✦ DIGGING DEEPER ✦

Even Jesus was willing to admit He was not the source of His own strength here on earth. He depended upon His Father for everything, and He gave God all the glory for what He was given to do. Take a look at a portion of Jesus' prayer in John 17:

"Now they have known that all things which You have given Me are from You. For I have given to them the words which You have given Me; and they have received them, and have known surely that I came forth from You; and they have believed that You sent Me." —vv. 7, 8

What did Jesus say God had given to Him? What did He do with what He had received? Did Jesus tell His disciples who the source of all these things was? And who was it?

✦ PONDER & PRAY ✦

Pray this week for God to show you how much you can depend upon Him. He is the source, the answer to your every need—including your desire for contentment in life. Thank God for all He has supplied.

✦ TRINKETS TO TREASURE ✦

A source is that thing from which something springs. God is the Source of your joy and your strength. Jesus is the Source of your life and your hope. The Spirit is the Source of your spiritual gifts. To help you remember all of this, the trinket for this week is a spring. Never forget the Source from which all of your contentment will spring.

✦ NOTES & PRAYER REQUESTS ✦

CHAPTER 10

EVEN IF...

"WHEN LIFE IS GOOD, ENJOY IT. BUT WHEN LIFE IS HARD,
REMEMBER; GOD GIVES GOOD TIMES AND HARD TIMES,
AND NO ONE KNOWS WHAT TOMORROW WILL BRING."

Ecclesiastes 7:14 NCV

♡

Ontentment is hard to hold on to in the face of unexpected glitches. What kind of day have you had lately? Life with a three year–old can bring you close to tears sometimes. Take some of my days lately.

My boy swallowed a marble so his big sister couldn't take it away from him. (We got it back a couple of days later.) He squirted ketchup all over my pantry floor. He pulled a bowl of peaches out of the refrigerator, got a spoon, and settled himself under the dining room table for a private picnic. He punched a hole in his bedroom wall by slamming the door repeatedly into it. One day, he pulled a chair up to the kitchen sink, turned the water on full blast, and started spraying the entire kitchen. By the

CLEARING
✦ THE ✦
COBWEBS

Is it easier to face
something hard,
if you know it
will be worth it
in the end?

time I arrived on the scene, there was a half–inch of water on the floor. He hides half–eaten food under the couch cushions, picks the locks on all the bedroom doors, draws on the walls, and is still in the process of peeling all the wallpaper off one section of the bathroom.

Every time I am confronted by these kinds of shenanigans, my contentment level is seriously threatened. I'm more likely to try pulling out my hair and wailing piteously. Fortunately, when you get to retell your story later, those tears rolling down your cheeks are accompanied by great big belly laughs.

1. Contentment is an attitude that shouldn't be ruffled by circumstances. What kind of perspective should we always have, according to Solomon in Ecclesiastes 9:9?

> *It is easy to believe that God can use our lives when we see immediate results, when positive feedback encourages us to press on. It is hard to keep walking when we see little sign that what we are doing is making a difference.*
>
> Sheila Walsh

"Each day is God's gift. It's all you get in exchange for the hard work of staying alive. Make the most of each one!" — MSG

2. What other advice does Solomon impart about life in Ecclesiastes 11:8?

3. The reality of life is that hard days do come. Holding onto contentment can be easier when you admit this to yourself. It's not as if Jesus didn't warn us it would be so. What did He tell His followers in John 16:33?

4. In 1 Peter 4:12, 13, how does Peter say we should react when trials come?

> *I have learned that pain has purpose, which, at the peak of excruciating discomfort, brings me little consolation. Hindsight, though, has often proven pain's value. In fact, I have found pain to be one of life's most effective teachers. It gains one's full attention. It takes lessons down to the bottom line.*
>
> Patsy Clairmont

5. In James 1:2, how does James say we should react when trials come?

When I picture myself in the perfect Christian walk, I see a woman who is patient and wise. She is completely faithful in studying the Word. She is committed to prayer. She always knows just what to do, what to say, and how to react. She is loving, compassionate, and confident in sharing her faith with others. My ideal life doesn't involve any bumps or scrapes. I'd really find it easier to be content if life would move along smoothly and without surprises. Wouldn't you think God would be pleased by those noble desires?

Actually, I don't think God is impressed with my daydreams. Wishing for perfection doesn't accomplish the LORD's work in me. He can use me, just as I am, so long as I am willing to be used. And all those trials I have to go through serve His purposes in making me grow into the person He wants me to become.

Nothing any of us experiences is pointless or useless. The good, the bad, the ugly, even the things we think will kill us—God uses it all, and He devises our destiny out of the stuff in our trash. He sifts it out, shows us the value, and then uses us to help others because of it.

Luci Swindoll

6. How long will our trials last? Do they serve any purpose? Check out 1 Peter 1:6, 7.

7. What can we learn from our problems, according to Romans 5:3?

8. When will our trials come to an end? Revelation 14:13 mentions that time.

9. Life is hard. That's a fact. But contentment is possible even if life gets complicated. Peace is possible even if we are surrounded by confusion. Joy is possible even if we don't know what to expect. What "even if" should we hang on to no matter what? It's in Isaiah 54:10.

✦ DIGGING DEEPER ✦

Psalm 18:18 says, "They confronted me in the day of my calamity, But the LORD was my support." How does God support us in tough times?

Take a look at these verses. Each tells a different way we are strengthened in trying times:

- Isaiah 41:10
- Luke 22:32
- Ephesians 3:16
- 2 Timothy 4:17

Whatever problems we're going through, they didn't come to stay; they "came to pass." And that helps us cope, whether it's cancer or problems in our marriages or with our children. We know that what's up ahead is going to be glorious because of the hope we have as Christians.

Barbara Johnson

✦ PONDER & PRAY ✦

In the days ahead, bring to mind the Scriptures in this lesson, especially on days when everything seems to be going wrong. Face each day with your eyes wide open, looking for what God has for you in each day—especially when those trials come. Pray that you will be teachable and ready to learn the lessons God wants you to understand. Pray you can learn to be content.

✦ TRINKETS TO TREASURE ✦

Whenever we think of the trials of life, we associate them with rocks—whether it's being stuck between a rock and a hard place, traveling a bumpy road, or having a pesky little pebble stuck inside your shoe. So this week's trinket is a little chip off that big, old block of hardships. God's purpose in our temporary discomfort is not to develop calluses that harden our hearts, but to strengthen us and inspire growth.

✦ Notes & Prayer Requests ✦

✦ NOTES & PRAYER REQUESTS ✦

CHAPTER 11

SATISFIED

"I WILL FORGET MY COMPLAINT; I WILL CHANGE THE LOOK ON MY FACE AND SMILE."

Job 9:27 NCV

♡

What do you say when you've had enough—when you are satisfied? As babies, we started out by burping, then later by learning to say, "All done." When we were a little older, we used "I'm full" to get out of eating our vegetables. Now, we push back from the table and say, "I couldn't eat another bite." We're sated, stuffed, bursting, jam-packed, chock full, crammed, filled to the gills, and full up. I love how my father-in-law always put it. "My sufficiency has been suffonsified and anything additional would be superfluous."

When we are satisfied with God, how do we behave ourselves? Do we keep trying to pile things on our plates? Do we

CLEARING ✦ THE ✦ COBWEBS

What kinds of foods do you find most satisfying—crunchy or chewy, salty or sweet, hot or cold?

keep taking just one more trip to the buffet? Do we look longingly towards the kitchen door, hoping something more will be forthcoming? Or do we lay down our fork, push back from the table, and give our heartfelt thanks for what has been provided?

1. There is only one thing that should be coming out of the mouth of a contented woman. What is that, according to Ephesians 5:4?

Starting each morning with an attitude of gratitude— no matter what the circumstances—can splash joy over the rest of your day.

Barbara Johnson

2. Cultivating contentment means being satisfied with your niche in life, trusting that God has everything under control, and focusing your attention on Jesus instead of others. But it also means learning to be grateful for what you have. What does Paul urge us to do in Colossians 3:15?

3. What kinds of things should we be grateful for? Let's start in 1 Timothy 1:12.

4. Paul thanks God for his fellow believers, "making mention of you always in my prayers" (Philem. 1:4). According to 1 Thessalonians 2:13, why was he so grateful?

> *Dear friend, embrace your day—this day—it is a gift. Take the LORD's hand. He will help you unwrap the day and then celebrate it. And His grace will be sufficient for any need you have.*
>
> Patsy Clairmont

5. All of us can be thankful for "His indescribable gift" (2 Cor. 9:15). How does Paul describe this in 2 Thessalonians 2:13?

*L*earning "please" and "thank you" starts at home, and it can start early. When my baby started to talk, the first few words were the usual ones: "Daddy," "Mama," "up," and "all done." But right along with those words, he also started saying "thank you." Of course, it came out more like "tankoo," but as soon as I realized what he was saying, I sat back with tears in my eyes. How precious to hand a one–year–old baby his juice cup and have him say, "Tankoo, Mama."

I'll bet God is equally pleased when we take the time to thank Him for the simplest of His gifts to us. We are His children, and He must take pleasure in our grateful

> *The whole purpose of my life is to become more like Christ. Therefore, everything—that would be everything—that comes into it, good or bad, can be used by Him to make me into the woman He has called me to be. Stupid arguments with my mother—in—law, canceled flights, long lines in grocery stores, illness— everything can be viewed as a gift.*
>
> Sheila Walsh

hearts, even if our humble praise comes out more like "tankoo."

6. What does 2 Corinthians 2:14 say we should give thanks to God for?

7. For what are we grateful, according to 1 Corinthians 15:57?

8. What does 1 Thessalonians 5:18 say is God's will for your life?

9. How long will we be thanking God, according to Psalm 30:12?

✦ Digging Deeper ✦

Remember Daniel in the Bible? What a guy! What a life—kidnapped as a boy, sent far from home, subject to enormous peer pressure, the object of petty jealousies and slander, weighed down with enormous responsibilities as a government official. Yet what was Daniel's attitude throughout? How did Daniel keep his heart satisfied—content—according to Daniel 6:10? Is this your custom as well?

✦ Ponder & Pray ✦

As you ponder these many Scriptures and pray this week, ask the LORD to give you a grateful heart. Take time to consider all the things you have to be grateful for, and then say thank you for them. This is a wonderful time to learn to be satisfied with whatever Jesus has given you.

It is mind-boggling to me that Jesus Christ lives in me. What a concept. The fact that He chooses to commingle with me in this way is unfathomable! The truth that I can be integrated and whole in Him both challenges and delights me.

Luci Swindoll

✦ Trinkets to Treasure ✦

Your little treasure for the week is a small plate. It will help you to remember that, no matter what is on your plate from one day to the next, you will always have enough to be satisfied. What's more, once you've cleaned your plate, never forget to say thank you to the One who provided it all.

✦ Notes & Prayer Requests ✦

CHAPTER 12

A NEW CREATURE

"A STUDENT SHOULD BE SATISFIED TO BECOME LIKE HIS TEACHER; A SERVANT SHOULD BE SATISFIED TO BECOME LIKE HIS MASTER"

Matthew 10:25 NCV

♡

o you garden? Those of us who do are aware of a very pertinent fact—cultivation is not a one-time event. You can't just turn a bit of dirt over, poke in a seed, and walk away. Cultivating a garden takes time, energy, sweat, and persistence. There's the planting, the watering, the warding off of pests, and there's the weeding. Of course, none of us really like weeding. In fact, many of us put a considerable amount of effort into eliminating the need to weed. My Dad has it down to a science. Starting in the spring, he'll till the ground, mark off the rows, and set up the fences. Then we'll go through and lay down newspaper that we've saved all winter long. Next comes a layer of straw. On top of

CLEARING
+ THE +
COBWEBS

If you could
change anything
in your life—
your spiritual
life—what would it be?

that, we set out old tires in even rows. The tires are filled with soil and fertilizer from the neighbor's cow pasture. In these, we plant all our melons and squashes. Without any large areas of soil exposed, weeds don't take root. It's great!

When it's the soil of our hearts under cultivation, the crop we're hoping to reap is contentment. The efforts we put in early will help prevent problems from cropping up later. A dependence on God as our only source of satisfaction, an attitude of thankfulness, and a trust that the LORD is working for our good—these keep the weeds of discontentment and complaining out of our lives. And in trying to please our Heavenly Father, we become new creatures.

> *Every day we must renew our minds. I don't think God means do not plan, do not look forward to days to come. I believe He means that right now is the only opportunity we have to live for Him. Treat this moment, right now, as if it's your last moment because it might be.*
>
> Thelma Wells

1. Read this passage in Romans, as it is translated by *The Message*:

Don't become so well-adjusted to your culture that you fit into it without even thinking. Instead, fix your attention on God. You'll be changed from the inside out. Readily recognize what he wants from you, and quickly respond to it. Unlike the culture around you, always dragging you down to its level of immaturity, God brings the best out of you, develops well-formed maturity in you. —Romans 12:2

To become the woman God wants you to be, willpower isn't enough. Gumption won't carry you through. In order to cultivate contentment, you must be changed. How does that change come about according to the passage above?

2. In 2 Corinthians 5:17, what does Paul tell us about our lives, once we become Christians?

3. We can't do it ourselves. We need divine assistance. The song goes, "Change my heart, O God; make it ever new. Change my heart, O God; may I be like You." Do you long to experience a transformation of the heart? David did. What did he pray in Psalm 51:10?

>
>
> *God never calls what He doesn't enable. I believe in striking out and watching Him work out the details. Once we start something, a momentum begins that propels us toward completion. But it takes really wanting to do it to get started. There's no drive–through breakthrough in life. Nothing of value can be had for nothing.*
>
> Luci Swindoll

4. Once the heart is clean, then everything that flows out of it will also be clean. Jesus commented on this truth Himself in the gospels. What does Matthew 12:34, 35 say about the relationship between the heart and the tongue?

5. Our transformation into a new and beautiful creature doesn't happen all at once. How does Paul describe the process in 2 Corinthians 3:18?

Can God work a miracle in our hearts? You bet He can! And it doesn't even have to be about something "big." Sometimes He shows us His power in little ways. For instance—I am not a dog person. All that panting and drooling and whining and shedding—Yuck! But God can change even the most stubborn heart, and mine was softened towards the canine species to the point where I told my husband I wanted to get a puppy. In fact, when we came home from the breeder's house, we were the proud owners of two dogs—Chihuahuas! I named them Timothy and Titus.

That might not seem like much of a miracle to anybody else, but for our family, this was amazing. What are the miracles you might be seeking? Do you long for forgiveness towards someone who has hurt you deeply? Perhaps you have a habit you long to break or a relationship that needs strengthening. Are you putting something off? Do you long to be more compassionate? Are you struggling to be more faithful in your responsibilities? No matter where you long to see newness and change, God can work in your heart to bring it to pass.

6. When we are seeking contentment in our lives—seeking to be changed into women who glorify God—we turn to the Word of God to find the way. What does Ephesians 4:21–24 say about this process?

7. We are being changed, day by day, often in miraculous ways. What is our end goal, according to Philippians 2:5?

> *Frankly, I love the fact that God has a plan for the future, for every tomorrow of my life on earth and beyond. Even though I can't figure it all out, he's got it wired. This reassures me that I'm loved and safe.*
>
> Luci Swindoll

8. How does Paul describe our transformed life in Colossians 3:10?

9. "He who has begun a good work in you will complete it until the day of Jesus Christ" (Phil. 1:6). Holding fast to that promise, we can be encouraged by Paul's benediction in 2 Corinthians 13:11.

> *Dear brothers and sisters, I close my letter with these last words: Rejoice. Change your ways. Encourage each other. Live in harmony and peace. Then the God of love and peace will be with you.* —NLT

How do Paul's last words here represent a life of contentment?

✦ DIGGING DEEPER ✦

The Scriptures are filled with admonitions, encouragements, and prayers concerning the heart. Those who follow God consistently plead with their Father in heaven to take their hearts, change them, and make them more like His. Here are several verses from the Psalms that all plead with the LORD to touch our hearts and make us new creatures:

- Psalm 10:17
- Psalm 27:8
- Psalm 51:17
- Psalm 90:12
- Psalm 26:2
- Psalm 28:7
- Psalm 86:11

✦ PONDER & PRAY ✦

This week as you pray, sum up the lessons of this entire guide, reviewing them in your mind and before your LORD. Ask Him to perform the kinds of miracles in your heart you will recognize as His hand in your life. Seek Him in His Word. Watch for His work. Take confidence in knowing you are being changed from glory to glory.

✦ TRINKETS TO TREASURE ✦

As a reminder that we have had a "veil removed so that we can be mirrors that brightly reflect the glory of the LORD" (2 Cor. 3:18 NLT), your trinket for this week is a small mirror. As such, we shine as new creatures—having been transformed from the inside out because of God's working in our hearts.

✦ NOTES & PRAYER REQUESTS ✦

_____

_____

_____

_____

_____

_____

_____

_____

_____

✦ Notes & Prayer Requests ✦

✦ SHALL WE REVIEW? ✦

Every chapter has added a new trinket to your treasure trove of memories. Let's remind ourselves of the lessons they hold for us!

1. A teddy bear.

A fuzzy reminder that our searching for something "just right" can be ended when we turn to God.

2. A potato chip.

An irresistible reminder that the good things in this life are just a foretaste of eternity. Our souls will never be satisfied with anything but Jesus.

3. Sweet tarts.

We all have a tendency to complain when life disappoints, but the sourness of our souls can be sweetened with the LORD's help.

4. A medicine dropper.

A woman who complains is as annoying as a constant dripping from a leaky faucet. Even small doses wear down those around us. We need to measure our words with love and peace and encouragement instead.

5. A pacifier.

The complaining we exhibit reveals the childishness of our hearts. When we find ourselves sulking, we need to pop in that pacifier and send up a desperate prayer for a change of heart.

6. A button.

A whimsical reminder that there are times when it's best to button our lips. Instead, we can pour out everything in our hearts and minds to the LORD—He is capable of helping us in our needs.

7. A lemon.

Your reaction to such a gift all depends upon your perspective. Will it cause you to pucker? Or will you find a way to turn it into something delicious? It all depends upon your attitude!

8. A blue highlighter.

Blue marking chalk helps a seamstress follow a pattern. When we pattern our life after Christ, we follow Him through God's Word. We can mark our journey of His pattern through the pages of our Bible with this blue highlighter.

9. A spring.

A source is something from which something else springs. This trinket is a reminder that God is the Source of so much in our lives—including our contentment.

10. A pebble.

A reminder of the trials in our lives, and that the rub they create in our hearts is not to harden and callous our hearts, but to strengthen our souls and inspire growth.

11. A plate.

Whatever is on your plate from day to day will always be enough to satisfy you. No matter what might be provided, never forget to say thank you.

12. A mirror.

We have been transformed into new creatures, from the inside out. When God is at work in our hearts, our lives are like mirrors, reflecting the glory of God.

✦ LEADER'S GUIDE ✦

Chapter 1

1. When our hearts are restless, we often chase an impulse without giving it much thought. We turn to activities, hoping that busyness will drive away our dissatisfaction. Possessions are a tempting, though temporary, salve for the restless heart. Sometimes we need a change of scenery: new furniture, new wallpaper, new paint, new fixtures, new bedspread, new curtains, or new patio furniture. Sometimes we try to reinvent ourselves, hoping our new look will put our restlessness to rest.

2. King Solomon was fond of riddles, and the answer to his question "What four things never say 'enough'?" is found in verse 16: "the grave, the barren womb, the earth that is not satisfied with water—And the fire." No matter how much stuff we cram into our lives, hoping it will fill that sense of lack, our need will be unmet. Our attempts to satisfy that craving for contentment will be as useless as finding enough water to dampen the desert sands once and for all, or providing enough fuel to sate the raging wildfire.

3. "He might live a thousand years twice over but not find contentment. And since he must die like everyone else—well, what's the use?" (Eccl. 6:6 NLT). Even in ancient times, men and women were grasping for more and more things, hoping it would assuage their feelings of discontentment.

4. "Everything God made is waiting with excitement for God to show his children's glory completely. Everything God made was changed to become useless, not by its own wish but because God wanted it and because all along there was this hope: that everything God made would be set free from ruin to have the freedom and glory that belong to God's children" (Rom. 8:19–21 NCV). In spite of the beauty of creation, sin set everything askew. Our world is described as "useless" and "ruined." Other translations use descriptions like futile, vain, corrupt, cursed, dead, decayed, and held back. How can we expect to live contentedly in such a place?

5. "Why spend your money on something that is not real food? Why work for something that doesn't really satisfy you? Listen closely to me, and you will eat what is good; your soul will enjoy the rich food that satisfies" (Is. 55:2 NCV). Never forget that, although this world is passing away, our souls have eternity ahead of them. Though physical things can never satisfy, God can nourish us spiritually.

6. "You satisfy me more than the richest of food. I will praise you with songs of joy" (Ps. 63:5 NLT). What we crave physically cannot compare to the richness of God's provisions. It's as if David is saying God is more satisfying than a bacon double cheeseburger with fries, or a wedge of cheesecake, or a hot fudge sundae, or a grande cappuccino with extra whipped cream on top. And because of God's deluxe care, David responds with praise and songs of joy.

7. "Satisfy us in the morning with your unfailing love, so we may sing for joy to the end of our lives" (Ps. 90:14 NLT). Contentment begins with God, and His unfailing love for us. When we are satisfied by God's love, our joy will last for the rest of our lives.

8. "Yes, I have loved you with an everlasting love; Therefore with lovingkindness I have drawn you" (Jer. 31:3). Or as *The Message* puts it, "I've never quit loving you and never will. Expect love, love, and more love!"

9. "Now hope does not disappoint, because the love of God has been poured out in our hearts by the Holy Spirit who was given to us" (Rom. 5:5). Life may disappoint us sometimes, but our Heavenly Father never will. No matter what life may bring, for the believer there is a happy ending in store.

Chapter 2

1. "O God, You are my God; Early will I seek You; My soul thirsts for You; My flesh longs for You in a dry and thirsty land Where there is no water" (Ps. 63:1). David's soul is irresistibly drawn to his LORD with intense longing. He describes himself as thirsty—parched, dried out, dehydrated, cotton–mouthed, panting. David declares he cannot live without God any better than he could live without water.

2. "My soul longs, yes, even faints for the courts of the LORD; My heart and my flesh cry out for the living God" (Ps. 84:2). We can know our Heavenly Father, and see His hand in our lives, but our souls long to see Him face to face. We yearn for His presence—to be with Him.

3. Jesus left no doubts when He declared, "In My Father's house are many mansions; if it were not so, I would have told you. I go to prepare a place for you. And if I go to prepare a place for you, I will come again and receive you to Myself, that where I am, there you may be also" (John 14:2, 3). Jesus is coming again, and we will join Him in the place He is preparing for us.

4. "Our citizenship is in heaven, from which we also eagerly wait for the Savior, the LORD Jesus Christ" (Phil. 3:20). We may live in this world, but we are not citizens here. Paul declares our true citizenship is in heaven, so no wonder we sometimes feel homesick in our souls. Our hearts should maintain an attitude of eager expectance as we await Jesus' return.

5. "Eye has not seen, nor ear heard, Nor have entered into the heart of man the things which God has prepared for those who love Him" (1 Cor. 2:9). Our new home in heaven will be beyond our wildest dreams—unimaginably wonderful, perfect, and suited to God's redeemed. When we are welcomed there, we'll feel right at home.

6. "For we who are in this tent groan, being burdened, not because we want to be unclothed, but further clothed, that mortality may be swallowed up by life" (1 Cor. 5:4). In *The Message*, a portion of this text in Corinthians reads, "Sometimes we can hardly wait to move—and so we cry out in frustration. Compared to what's coming, living conditions around here seem like a stopover in an unfurnished shack, and we're tired of it! We've been given a glimpse of the real thing, our true home, our resurrection bodies!" (1 Cor. 5:2).

7. "For we know that the whole creation groans and labors with birth pangs together until now. Not only that, but we also who have the firstfruits of the Spirit, even we ourselves groan within ourselves, eagerly waiting for the adoption, the redemption of our body" (Rom. 8:22, 23).

8. "And God will wipe away every tear from their eyes; there shall be no more death, nor sorrow, nor crying. There shall be no more pain, for the former things have passed away" (Rev. 21:4). We shall bid farewell to earthly sorrows forever. "And there shall be no more curse, but the throne of God and of the Lamb shall be in it, and His servants shall serve Him" (Rev. 22:3). What's more, the curse of sin will be lifted. Sin will be no more. And all of us who belong to Jesus will be there to serve Him.

9. "Because I have done what is right, I will see you. When I awake, I will be fully satisfied, for I will see you face to face" (Ps. 17:15 NLT). Our contentment will be complete when we wake in glory and can see our LORD face to face.

Chapter 3

1. Other people's driving techniques, your cooking, young people today, finding time, paying taxes, men in general, mothers–in–law, the weather, rising prices, office politics, computer glitches, mosquitoes, criminal activity. You name it, and people can find a way to complain about it!

2. People complain for various reasons—to call attention to another's faults, to vent some personal frustration, to put someone else down, to point out some unfairness, to be contrary, or just out of habit. Complaining only serves to sour the mood in group settings. Most often, no purpose is served in drawing people's attention to faults and failures.

3. "Stone is heavy, and sand is weighty, but a complaining fool is worse than either" (Prov. 27:3 NCV). Complaining is hard to put up with. It's more oppressive than trying to lift a boulder, or to drag around a sack full of sand. What's more, Solomon calls the complainer a fool.

4. "My soul loathes my life; I will give free course to my complaint, I will speak in the bitterness of my soul" (Job 10:1). Job doesn't want to hold anything back. With so much hurt and bitterness in his soul, he simply must get it all out. He gives free reign to the words built up inside of him.

5. "People complain when there is no salt in their food. And how tasteless is the uncooked white of an egg!" (Job 6:6 NLT). No salt for his eggs. Now that's taking a pretty dismal outlook on life!

6. Many times, when a woman complains, she isn't even thinking about what she says. Some of us were raised in homes where complaining took up the bulk of family conversation! Since so many women make these little, disgruntled comments in every situation, it really has become a form of small talk. It's a thoughtless habit. We blurt out what we think without screening it through our brains and considering the fact that we have become complainers.

7. "When they got their coin, they complained to the man who owned the land" (Matt. 20:11 NCV). Though the workmen received exactly what they had been promised, they compared their circumstances to those of the other workers. With a wail of "unfair!" they complained to the landowner in hopes of receiving more money. Their pursuits are like those of the men described in Job 20:20, "Such God–denying people are never content with what they have or who they are; their greed drives them relent-lessly" (Job 20:20 MSG).

8. "Do not consider your maidservant a wicked woman, for out of the abundance of my complaint and grief I have spoken until now" (1 Sam. 1:16). Hannah was in the Temple, pouring out her troubles to God in prayer. She was hurting because of the taunting of a family member and because she had been unable to bear a child. Her prayers would have been unheard by another soul, had not Eli discovered her in her petition.

9. God welcomed Hannah's prayers and answered her complaints by giving her the children she longed for. God listened to all of Job's bitterness, answered him, and then blessed him more abundantly than ever before. When you bring your complaints to God, He is patient to listen, and He can do something about them! When you bring your little snips and quibbles up to those around you, they may listen patiently, but that is all they can do. All your grumbling may serve to vent your soul, but your words remain in the minds of your listeners, sour the atmosphere around you, and stir up a willingness in your friends to return the favor—and dump all *their* complaints onto you. What a vicious cycle!

Chapter 4

1. This woman is quarrelsome (NCV), bothersome (NCV), nagging (MSG), annoying (NLT), contentious (NKJV), leaky (MSG), and drip, drip, drippy (MSG).

2. Children take their cues from the adults. When Mom is tense, irritable, and volatile, those around her behave similarly. When mama ain't happy, ain't nobody happy! On the other hand, when Mom remains calm, speaks courteously, and radiates contentment, her family learns to echo these qualities. When a woman is able to set the temperature in her home in this way, she creates a haven of peace for her family.

3. "It is better to live alone in the desert than with a crabby, complaining wife" (Prov. 21:19 NLT). If you are married, does your husband sometimes long for a quiet, desert retreat?

4. All of us get to grousing now and then. If we were really honest with ourselves, we'd all admit that we don't *want* to be complainers.

5. Complainers make tiresome companions. They are never satisfied, never happy, never complimentary, and never grateful. Be careful that you don't exhaust your friends and family by constantly unloading on them. They won't like it any more than you would!

6. "He who walks with wise men will be wise, but the companion of fools will be destroyed" (Prov. 13:20). Choosing your friends is just as important now as it was when you were young.

7. "Friends, don't complain about each other. A far greater complaint could be lodged against you. The Judge is standing just around the corner" (James 5:9 MSG). Don't grumble about your brothers and sisters in the LORD. God could condemn you for the same things, and more, if He were to bring you before the Judge.

8. "I call to remembrance the genuine faith that is in you, which dwelt first in your grandmother Lois and your mother Eunice, and I am persuaded is in you also" (1 Tim. 1:5). Here are two women of faith who turned their abilities towards raising up a boy into a godly man.

9. "As each one has received a gift, minister it to one another, as good stewards of the manifold grace of God" (1 Pet. 4:10). Use your gift to share grace, to spread love, and to serve.

Chapter 5

1. "They began to murmur against God and Moses. 'Why have you brought us out of Egypt to die here in the wilderness?' they complained. 'There is nothing to eat here and nothing to drink. And we hate this wretched manna!'" (Num. 21:5 NLT). The people were in a snit, and their complaint had no real truth behind it. They said they had nothing to eat, yet in the next breath they complained about the manna God had provided for them to eat.

2. "In the morning you will see the Glory of God. Yes, he's listened to your complaints against him. You haven't been complaining against us, you know, but against God" (Ex. 16:7 MSG). When we lash out because we don't like our lives, our complaints are heard in heaven. In a sense, we are telling God He's not doing things right, and we want Him to do things our way.

3. "Do not test the LORD your God as you did when you complained" (Deut. 6:6 NLT). "So once more the people grumbled and complained to Moses…Moses replied, 'Why are you arguing with me? And why are you testing the LORD?'" (Ex. 17:2 NLT). In both verses, the complainers are said to be testing God.

4. "Now when the people complained, it displeased the LORD; for the LORD heard it, and His anger was aroused. So the fire of the LORD burned among them, and consumed some in the outskirts of the camp" (Num. 11:1).

5. "You will eat it for a whole month until you gag and are sick of it. For you have rejected the LORD, who is here among you, and you have complained to him, 'Why did we ever leave Egypt?'" (Num. 11:20 NLT).

6. "You will die in this desert. Every one of you who is twenty years old or older and who was counted with the people—all of you who complained against me—will die" (Num. 14:29 NCV). The New King James Version is even more graphic: "The carcasses of you who have complained against Me shall fall in the wilderness."

7. Selfish, ungrateful, forgetful, cantankerous, rebellious, argumentative, childish, peevish, changeable.

8. "Why would you ever complain, O Jacob, or, whine, Israel, saying, 'God has lost track of me. He doesn't care what happens to me?'" (Is. 40:27 MSG). The prophet's tone is almost incredulous. How could God's people complain? You are His chosen ones. He has shown you great love. Look at all He has done for you!

9. God knows you. He loves you. He has chosen you for His own. He came for you. He died for you. He cares for you. He has given you an eternal hope. No matter what inconveniences you face on this earth, you are assured of living "happily ever after."

Chapter 6

1. "A fool vents all his feelings, but a wise man holds them back" (Prov. 29:11). As we've mentioned before, venting is fine, so long as it is directed to our LORD. Tell it all to Him. But if you are wise, you will hold back and curb your tongue when others are around.

2. The *New King James Version* reads "Be angry, and do not sin. Meditate with your heart on your bed, and be still" (Ps. 4:4). However, *The Message* renders it, "Complain if you must, but don't lash out. Keep your mouth shut, and let your heart do the talking" (Ps. 4:4). This seems to be saying that if you have complaints, you should hold your tongue and let your heart do the talking. This will keep you from sinning.

3. "Whoever guards his mouth and tongue keeps his soul from troubles" (Prov. 21:23). When we get frustrated, it becomes even more important to watch our mouths.

4. "For we all stumble in many things. If anyone does not stumble in word, he is a perfect man, able also to bridle the whole body" (James 3:2). Nobody is perfect, and so we all end up saying things we wish we hadn't. That leads us into trouble—sin.

5. No. You can't fake contentment.

6. "Those in error will then believe the truth, and those who constantly complain will accept instruction." (Is. 29:24 NLT). *The Message* puts it this way: "Those who got off–track will get back on–track, and complainers and whiners learn gratitude." In order to put complaining behind you, you must be willing to accept instruction—that means being teachable, moldable, willing to change. What's more, the complainer in all of us needs to learn gratitude. When you keep in mind everything for which you are thankful, you'll have nothing to complain about!

7. "Actually, I don't have a sense of needing anything personally. I've learned by now to be quite content whatever my circumstances" (Phil. 4:11 MSG). Just like the rest of us, Paul had to *learn* how to be content.

8. "Now godliness with contentment is great gain" (1 Tim. 6:6). Contentment elevates the godly life to one of pricelessness.

9. Like the old song goes, "Love and marriage…You can't have one without the other!" Perhaps the same is true about godliness and contentment. A godly life is made all the richer by finding satisfaction in it. And who would *want* to find contentment in a life that was anything but pleasing in God's eyes?

Chapter 7

1. Some people are better than others at hanging on to hope when the storm clouds come rolling in. Being able to perceive the silver lining on the blackest of clouds is a gift. Those who have it—the ability to take hold of faith no matter what comes—must share it. These are the encouragers God has put among us.

2. "'For I know the plans I have for you,' says the LORD. 'They are plans for good and not for disaster, to give you a future and a hope'" (Jer. 29:11 NLT). You can be content with your life and your future, knowing God has plans for your life and He has given you hope.

3. "Count it all joy when you fall into various trials, knowing that the testing of your faith produces patience. But let patience have its perfect work, that you may be perfect and complete, lacking nothing" (James 1:2–4). You can be content even when life throws you a curve, because you know God's hand is over you, and He is teaching you something that will help to perfect and complete you.

4. "You meant evil against me; but God meant it for good" (Gen. 50:20). When you were a kid, were you ever told you have to do something because "it's for your own good?" If everything in life that happens to us can be used by God for our own good, then shouldn't we trust Him?

5. "And it is a good thing to receive wealth from God and the good health to enjoy it. To enjoy your work and accept your lot in life—that is indeed a gift from God. People who do this rarely look with sorrow on the past, for God has given them reasons for joy" (Eccl. 5:19, 20 NLT).

6. "Job's wife said to him, 'Why are you trying to stay innocent? Curse God and die!' Job answered, 'You are talking like a foolish woman. Should we take only good things from God and not trouble?' In spite of all this Job did not sin in what he said" (Job 2:9, 10 NCV). Despite the fact that Job had lost his children, his wealth, and now his health, he refused to lash out against God for it. Job holds on to his integrity when he holds on to his tongue.

7. "A meal of bread and water in contented peace is better than a banquet spiced with quarrels" (Prov. 17:1 MSG). Be content with what you have, even if it doesn't seem like much.

8. "Though the fig tree may not blossom, Nor fruit be on the vines; Though the labor of the olive may fail, And the fields yield no food; Though the flock may be cut off from the fold, And there be no herd in the stalls—Yet I will rejoice in the LORD, I will joy in the God of my salvation. The LORD God is my strength; He will make my feet like deer's feet, And He will make me walk on my high hills" (Hab. 3:17–19).

9. "Be kindly affectionate to one another with brotherly love, in honor giving preference to one another; not lagging in diligence, fervent in spirit, serving the LORD; rejoicing in hope, patient in tribulation, continuing steadfastly in prayer; distributing to the needs of the saints, given to hospitality. Bless those who persecute you; bless and do not curse. Rejoice with those who rejoice, and weep with those who weep. Be of the same mind toward one another. Do not set your mind on high things, but associate with the humble. Do not be wise in your own opinion. Repay no one evil for evil. Have regard for good things in the sight of all men. If it is possible, as much as depends on you, live peaceably with all men" (Rom. 12:10–18). Don't just sit and soak in your contentment. God gives us His perspective on life so we can see the needs of others and show them His love.

Chapter 8

1. "I am just like you before God; I too am made out of clay." No matter how much renown some women have gained, no matter how impressive their resumes have become, they are just like us. We are all forgiven, we are all sisters, and we all serve the same Savior. No one is better than the other, we just carry out different roles in the Body.

2. Paul has put all else aside and given Jesus the highest priority in his life. To what end? "That I may gain Christ and be found in Him…that I may know Him and the power of His resurrection…if, by any means, I may attain to the resurrection from the dead" (Phil. 3:8–11). Paul has eternity in view. Verse 15 in *The Message* reads: "So let's keep focused on that goal, those of us who want everything God has for us. If any of you have something else in mind, something less than total commitment, God will clear your blurred vision—you'll see it yet!"

3. "Focus on reading the Scriptures to the church, encouraging the believers, and teaching them" (1 Tim. 4:13 NLT). The Scriptures are our main source of teaching and encouragement. If you want to keep your eyes focused on Jesus so you can live contentedly, you must not neglect the Word!

4. "We have the prophetic word made more sure, which you do well to heed as a light that shines in a dark place, until the day dawns and the morning star rises in your hearts" (2 Pet. 1:19). Our Bibles are our only true source of light until Christ returns for us. As Peter says, we would do well to take heed!

5. "I concentrate on doing exactly what You say—I always have and always will" (Ps. 119:112 MSG). Read the Word, and act on what you find there. It may take concentration on your part, but that's how David came to be known as a man after God's own heart!

6. "Don't let them depart from your eyes; keep them in the midst of your heart" (Prov. 4:21). In *The Message*, Solomon urges us to keep the Word "in plain view at all times. Concentrate! Learn it by heart!" It isn't enough to simply read your Bible. The wise man encourages us to commit the Scriptures to memory.

7. "When you do things, do not let selfishness or pride be your guide. Instead, be humble and give more honor to others than to yourselves" (Phil. 2:3 NCV). Even if we keep our eyes off other people, we can get into trouble by keeping our eyes firmly fixed on ourselves! Then, as James puts it, "where self-seeking exists, confusion and every evil thing are there" (James 3:16).

8. "Long before he laid down earth's foundations, he had us in mind, had settled on us as the focus of his love, to be made whole and holy by his love" (Eph. 1:4 MSG). You are loved! Keep your attention focused on the lover of your soul.

9. "For I have given you an example, that you should do as I have done to you." (John 13:15). If we have any questions as to how we should be living, we can always go back to Christ, for He set us an example for godly living.

Chapter 9

1. "The LORD is the source of all my righteousness and strength" (Is. 45:24 NLT). Other versions translate this as "goodness and power" (NCV), and "salvation and strength" (MSG). Jesus has saved us from sin, and He gives us the strength we need for living.

2. "I will go to the altar of God, to God—the source of all my joy" (Ps. 43:4 NLT). God gives us joy. Joy is a definite contentment booster!

3. "Your Word is my only source of hope" (Ps. 119:114 NLT). How else would we know of God's promises to us, if we didn't have His Word to study? Hope—another good foundation for the contented life!

4. "All praise to the God and Father of our LORD Jesus Christ. He is the source of every mercy and the God who comforts us" (2 Cor. 1:3 NLT). Mercy and comfort are ours because of our Heavenly Father.

5. "Now there are different kinds of spiritual gifts, but it is the same Holy Spirit who is the source of them all" (1 Cor. 12:4 NLT). God, through His Holy Spirit, has equipped you with the special abilities you need in order to serve Him effectively. We can be content, knowing God has fitted us for the tasks He will set before us.

6. When days get rough, we often try to content ourselves with quick fixes: a little snack (comfort food!), an hour or two of escape via the television, some heavy–duty housekeeping to get our minds off things, shoe shopping, a trip to the scrap–booking store, or maybe playing Solitaire on the computer. We all have ways and places we fall back on, when we should be turning to the true Source—God.

7. "Speaking the truth with love, we will grow up in every way into Christ, who is the head. The whole body depends on Christ, and all the parts of the body are joined and held together. Each part does its own work to make the whole body grow and be strong with love" (Eph. 4:15, 16 NCV). Jesus is the head of the Church—the Leader, the source of life, strength, and guidance. *The Message* interprets a portion of that passage, "We take our lead from Christ, who is the source of everything we do."

8. "The Head, from whom all the body, nourished and knit together by joints and ligaments, grows with the increase that is from God" (Col. 2:19). Paul says Jesus binds us together with other believers, and He nourishes us. That is the only way we can remain spiritually healthy—by staying connected to Jesus, the Head.

9. Isaiah indicates God is the source of our contentment—"all we'll ever want"— because of who He is and what He has done. Because of this, we do not rush from His side or His way. We choose instead to linger in His presence. We trust His decisions for our life, content that they are the very best things.

Chapter 10

1. Solomon's wise word for us is to make the most of every day.

2. "Even if you live a long time, don't take a single day for granted. Take delight in each light–filled hour, remembering that there will also be many dark days and that most of what comes your way is smoke" (Eccl. 11:8 MSG). Solomon's advice is to never take the good times for granted, and remember dark days come to all of us. No matter what happens, every day is a gift.

3. "I have told you all this so that you may have peace in Me. Here on earth you will have many trials and sorrows. But take heart, because I have overcome the world" (John 16:33 NLT). We were never guaranteed sunny skies and smooth sailing. Jesus gave fair warning that trials would be a big part of the life of anyone that belonged to Him.

4. "Dear friends, don't be surprised at the fiery trials you are going through, as if something strange were happening to you. Instead, be very glad—because these trials will make you partners with Christ in his suffering, and afterward you will have the wonderful joy of sharing his glory when it is displayed to all the world" (1 Pet. 4:12, 13 NLT). First of all, don't be surprised. Secondly, be glad, because people are treating you just like they treated Jesus.

5. "Count it all joy when you fall into various trials" (James 1:2). James echoes Peter in urging us to face our trials with joy.

6. "In this you greatly rejoice, though now for a little while, if need be, you have been grieved by various trials, that the genuineness of your faith, being much more precious than gold that perishes, though it is tested by fire, may be found to praise, honor, and glory at the revelation of Jesus Christ" (1 Pet. 1:6, 7).

7. "We can rejoice, too, when we run into problems and trials, for we know that they are good for us—they help us learn to endure" (Rom. 5:3 NLT). Our trials teach us how to endure.

8. "Blessed are those who die in the LORD from now on. Yes, says the Spirit, they are blessed indeed, for they will rest from all their toils and trials; for their good deeds follow them!" (Rev. 14:13). Basically, we won't get a rest from our trials until we die, or until the LORD returns—whichever comes first.

9. No matter what we face in our lives, we can hang onto the fact that we are loved, loved, loved! God's covenant will stand. We will make it in the end.

Chapter 11

1. "Neither filthiness, nor foolish talking, nor coarse jesting, which are not fitting, but rather giving of thanks" (Eph. 5:4). Our mouths should be filled with praise and thanksgiving.

2. "Let the peace of God rule in your hearts…and be thankful" (Col. 3:15). Peace and contentment can only be found in a heart that is aware and thankful for what God has provided.

3. "I thank Christ Jesus our LORD who has enabled me, because He counted me faithful, putting me into the ministry" (1 Tim. 1:12). Paul announces he is thankful for Jesus' choosing him to serve in the ministry, and for enabling him to do the task set before him.

4. "For this reason we also thank God without ceasing, because when you received the word of God which you heard from us, you welcomed it not as the word of men, but as it is in truth, the word of God, which also effectively works in you who believe" (1 Thess. 2:13). Paul is thankful because those who have read his letters recognized them as the very Word of God, and were changed when they acted upon its truth.

5. "We are bound to give thanks to God always for you, brethren beloved by the LORD, because God from the beginning chose you for salvation through sanctification by the Spirit and belief in the truth" (2 Thess. 2:13). Paul is thankful at all times for the very gift of salvation that was his. He also appreciated the sanctifying work of the Spirit in his life, and the truth (God's Word) he believed.

6. "Now thanks be to God who always leads us in triumph in Christ, and through us diffuses the fragrance of His knowledge in every place" (2 Cor. 2:14). We should be thankful God leads us, where He leads us is triumph, and He touches the world through us.

7. "But thanks be to God, who gives us the victory through our LORD Jesus Christ" (1 Cor. 15:57). We can be grateful because through Jesus, we will be victorious.

8. "In everything give thanks, for this is the will of God in Christ Jesus for you" (1 Thess. 5:18). Amazing! It is God's will for your life that you be thankful.

9. "To the end that my glory may sing praise to You and not be silent. O LORD my God, I will give thanks to You forever" (Ps. 30:12). We will never stop thanking God for all His love and mercy and grace. Even in Revelation, the scene in heaven describes thanksgiving: "We give You thanks, O LORD God Almighty, The One who is and who was and who is to come" (Rev. 11:17).

Chapter 12

1. "Do not be conformed to this world, but be transformed by the renewing of your mind, that you may prove what is that good and acceptable and perfect will of God" (Rom. 12:2). God is in the process of making us who He wants us to be, and He is the one doing the work—from the inside out. What is required of us is to recognize His hand and respond to His leading.

2. "If anyone is in Christ, he is a new creation; old things have passed away; behold, all things have become new" (2 Cor. 5:17). We aren't slaves to our old ways of doing things—our familiar habits of searching, selfishness, and complaining. We have been made new. "In Christ Jesus…a new creation" (Gal. 6:15).

3. "Create in me a clean heart, O God, and renew a steadfast spirit within me" (Ps. 51:10). David wanted to be new, and that kind of change can only happen from the inside out. The heart is where God works His first and best miracles in our lives.

4. "Brood of vipers! How can you, being evil, speak good things? For out of the abundance of the heart the mouth speaks. A good man out of the good treasure of his heart brings forth good things, and an evil man out of the evil treasure brings forth evil things" (Matt. 12:34, 35). When God has been at work in your heart, it shows by what comes out of your mouth. Harsh words and complaints betray a heart that has wandered away from the LORD. When we welcome Jesus' transforming power in our souls, His love and joy brim over, spilling out in our words.

5. "We all, with unveiled face, beholding as in a mirror the glory of the LORD, are being transformed into the same image from glory to glory, just as by the Spirit of the LORD" (2 Cor. 3:18). When we spend time considering the glory of our LORD, we can't help but be changed so we are more and more like Him. It happens little by little, glory to glory.

6. "I know that you heard about him, and you are in him, so you were taught the truth that is in Jesus. You were taught to leave your old self—to stop living the evil way you lived before. That old self becomes worse, because people are fooled by the evil things they want to do. But you were taught to be made new in your hearts, to become a new person. That new person is made to be like God—made to be truly good and holy" (Eph. 4:21–24 NCV). From this passage, we learn a few different things. Jesus taught the truth, and we need to know it. We can learn from Jesus' example, and emulate Him. We can change, leaving our old selves behind and being made into new, good, and holy people.

7. "In your lives you must think and act like Christ Jesus" (Phil. 2:5 NCV). We are being changed, little by little, into the likeness of the LORD we serve. We want to be like Jesus. As stated in Matthew 10:25, "A student should be satisfied to become like his teacher; a servant should be satisfied to become like his master" (NCV).

8. We have "put on the new man, who is renewed in knowledge according to the image of Him who created him" (Col. 3:10). Contentment has to be learned, and the new man has to be put on! I love *The Message's* description of this passage: "Now you're dressed in a new wardrobe. Every item of your new way of life is custom-made by the Creator, with his label on it. All the old fashions are now obsolete." Have you cleaned out your closet, making room for God's custom designs for your heart?

9. "Be cheerful. Keep things in good repair. Keep your spirits up. Think in harmony. Be agreeable. Do all that, and the God of love and peace will be with you for sure" (2 Cor. 13:11 MSG). Paul's summary statement seems to be a good description of the contented life: thankfulness, teachability, encouragement, peace, harmony, and closeness to God.

✦ Acknowledgments ✦

© Clairmont, Patsy, *The Best Devotions of Patsy Clairmont,* (Grand Rapids, MI: Zondervan Publishing House, 2001)

© Johnson, Barbara, *Daily Splashes of Joy,* (Nashville, TN: W Publishing Group, 2000)

© Johnson, Nicole, *Fresh–Brewed Life: A Stirring Invitation to Wake up Your Soul,* (Nashville, TN: Thomas Nelson, Inc., 2001)

© Johnson, Nicole, *Keeping a Princess Heart in a Not–So–Fairy–Tale World,* (Nashville, TN: W Publishing Group, 2003)

© Meberg, Marilyn, *The Best Devotions of Marilyn Meberg* (Grand Rapids, MI: Zondervan Publishing House, 2001)

© Swindoll, Luci, *I Married Adventure* (Nashville, TN: W Publishing Group, 2003)

© Walsh, Sheila, *The Best Devotions of Sheila Walsh and Unexpected Grace* (Grand Rapids, MI: Zondervan Publishing House, 2001)

© Wells, Thelma, *The Best Devotions of Thelma Wells* (Grand Rapids, MI: Zondervan Publishing House, 2001)

✦ Statement of Faith ✦

Women of Faith believes...

The Bible to be the inspired, the only infallible, inerrant Word of God.

There is one God, eternally existent in three persons: Father, Son, and Holy Spirit.

He has revealed Himself in creation, history and Jesus Christ.

God's creation of the world and humankind with humanity's rebellion and subsequent depravity.

In the person and work of Jesus Christ, including His deity,

His virgin birth, His sinless life, His true humanity, His miracles,

His substitutionary death, His bodily resurrection,

His ascension to heaven, and His personal return in power and glory.

That for salvation of the lost, sinful man, regeneration by the Holy Spirit is absolutely essential.

Salvation is by grace through faith in Christ as one's Savior.

In the present ministry of the Holy Spirit by whose indwelling the Christian is enabled to live a godly life and to grow in the knowledge of God and Christian obedience.

In the resurrection of both the saved and the lost—the saved unto the resurrection of life and the lost unto the resurrection of damnation.

In the spiritual unity of believers in the LORD Jesus Christ and in the importance of church for worship, service and missions.

✦ NOTES ✦

✦ Notes ✦

✦ NOTES ✦

✦ NOTES ✦

✦ Notes ✦

✦ NOTES ✦

✦ Notes ✦

✦ NOTES ✦

WOMEN OF FAITH®
A Division of Thomas Nelson, Inc.

PRESENTS

Irrepressible
HOPE
CONFERENCE 2004

Featured Speakers & Dramatist:

Sheila Walsh

Marilyn Meberg

Luci Swindoll

Patsy Clairmont

Thelma Wells

Nicole Johnson

There is more to life than just staying afloat!
Experience the all-new two day conference that can put fresh wind in your sails — with stirring music, engaging dramatic presentations and refreshing messages.

We have this hope as an anchor for the soul, firm and secure.
—HEBREWS 6:19

2004 Event Cities and Special Guests

Shreveport, LA
February 27-28
CenturyTel Center

Philadelphia, PA - I
March 5-6
Wachovia Spectrum

San Antonio, TX*
March 18-20
AlamoDome

Ft. Wayne, IN
March 26-27
Allen County
War Memorial
Coliseum- Arena

Spokane, WA
April 16-17
Spokane Arena

Cincinnati, OH
April 23-24
US Bank Arena

San Jose, CA
May 7-8
HP Pavilion

Nashville, TN
May 14-15
Gaylord Entertainment
Center

Charleston, SC
May 21-22
N. Charleston Coliseum

Des Moines, IA
June 4-5
Veterans Memorial
Auditorium

Anaheim, CA - I
June 18-19
Arrowhead Pond

Pittsburgh, PA
June 25-26
Mellon Arena

Denver, CO
July 9-10
Pepsi Center

Ft. Lauderdale, FL
July 16-17
Office Depot Center

St. Louis, MO
July 23-24
Savvis Center

Atlanta, GA
July 30-31
Philips Arena

Washington, DC
August 6-7
MCI Center

Buffalo, NY
August 13-14
HSBC Arena

Omaha, NE
August 20-21
Qwest Center Omaha

Dallas, TX
August 27-28
American Airlines Center

Anaheim, CA - II
September 10-11
Arrowhead Pond

Albany, NY
September 17-18
Pepsi Arena

Philadelphia, PA - II
September 24-25
Wachovia Center

Hartford, CT
October 1-2
Hartford Civic Center

Portland, OR
October 8-9
Rose Garden Arena

Orlando, FL
October 15-16
TD Waterhouse Centre

St. Paul, MN
October 22-23
Xcel Energy Center

Charlotte, NC
October 29-30
Charlotte Coliseum

Oklahoma City, OK
November 5-6
Ford Center

Vancouver, BC
November 12-13
GM Place

Dates and locations subject to change.

* Special National Conference. Call 1-888-49-FAITH for details.

For more information call **1-888-49-FAITH** or visit **womenoffaith.com**

The Complete *Women of Faith*® Study Guide Series

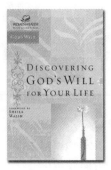

Discovering God's
Will for Your Life
0-7852-4983-4

Living Above
Worry and Stress
0-7852-4986-9

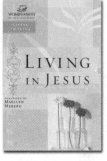

Living in Jesus
0-7852-4985-0

Adventurous
Prayer
0-7852-4984-2

New Releases

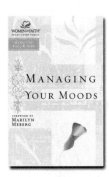

Managing
Your Moods
0-7852-5151-0

Cultivating
Contentment
0-7852-5152-9

Encouraging
One Another
0-7852-5153-7

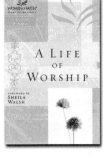

A Life of Worship
0-7852-5154-5

WOMEN OF FAITH®

A Message of Grace & Hope
for Every Day

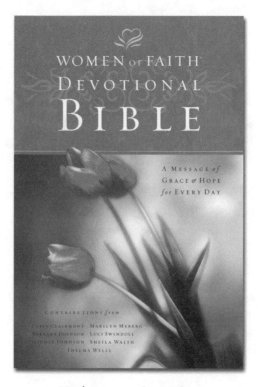

Hardcover: 0-7180-0378-0
Paperback: 0-7180-0377-2
Bonded Leather: 0-7180-0379-9

The *Women of Faith® Devotional Bible* provides women with the inspiration and resources needed to strengthen their walk with God and build stronger relationships with others. It helps women of all ages and stages in life – mature believers and those who have yet to believe, from all backgrounds, church and non-churched — to grow spiritually, emotionally, and relationally.